the best
pressure cooker
recipes on the planet

200 Triple-Tested, Family-Approved,
Fast & Easy Recipes

DEBRA MURRAY

Castle Point Books
New York

THE BEST PRESSURE COOKER RECIPES ON THE PLANET

www.castlepointbooks.com
www.stmartins.com

ISBN: 978-1-250-09613-5 (paperback)

Photography courtesy of Allan Penn and Shutterstock.com.
Book design by Claire MacMaster, barefoot art graphic design

Our books may be purchased in bulk for promotional,
educational, or business use. Please contact your local
bookseller or the Macmillan Corporate and Premium
Sales Department at 1-800-221-7945, extension 5442,
or by e-mail at MacmillanSpecialMarkets@macmillan.com.

First Edition: October 2016

10 9 8 7 6 5 4 3 2 1

This book is dedicated to my precious late husband, Martin,
whose belief in and love for me
gave me the courage to go after my dreams.

*

I would never have been able to write this book of my dreams
without my friend Bruce Lubin, and my best friend, Laurie Bain,
who helped me type and test every one of these recipes.

172 CHAPTER SIX ✳ Side Dishes

207 CHAPTER SEVEN ✳ Grains & Pastas

236 CHAPTER EIGHT ✳ Desserts

Introduction

I ADORE PRESSURE COOKERS! I love the speed, the ease, and how nutritious the food is, but mostly I'm obsessed with the clean and intense flavors that a pressure cooker gives you. I've been enchanted by pressure cooking since my first experience with a pressure cooker over fifteen years ago. One bite of pot roast and I became a loyal fan. It reminded me of the beautiful food my grandmother lovingly fed us when I was growing up. Now, with a pressure cooker, you can have Sunday dinners seven nights a week, in a snap!

When pressure-cooking, the cooking liquid comes to a boil when it reaches 212°F. At that point, the liquid is converted to vapor (or steam). When the steam is prevented from escaping, it raises the temperature of the liquid by 40°F. That alone would help cut back on the normal cooking time, but the steam molecules break down the surface tension of whatever you are cooking and infuse the food with the rich flavors of the stock or sauce in minutes.

Another attribute of pressure-cooking is that each steam molecule is a water molecule expanded enormously, so you need less sodium when cooking—a perfect way to reduce your salt intake. Lean pieces of meat like London broil can be as tender as butter in under an hour. This lowers your fat servings without sacrificing flavor.

When cooking with a pressure cooker, you will find time-savings of up to 70 percent. In some cases, food cooks faster in a pressure cooker than in a microwave, but with much better texture and nutrient retention.

I make everything quick and easy—one-pot pasta from dry noodles and frozen protein to rice and beans and meats. However, my hands-down favorites are the stocks and soups.

I have shared two hundred recipes here to start you down the road to pressure-cooking. If you don't already love pressure-cooking, you obviously have never tried it! This book will play Cupid in your new affair with pressure-cooking.

I have written this book so you can cook with either an electric pressure cooker or with a stovetop pressure cooker. If you are using an electric pressure cooker, you will just set the pressure cooker for the specific amount of time indicated in the recipe. You will not have to wait for it to come to pressure. Most electric pressure cookers, even though many have lots of buttons, maintain the same temperature. So do not worry about which function to press; you need only make sure that the function will allow for the length of time I have specified.

For stovetop pressure-cooking, you can set the stove temperature to medium-high to bring it to temperature, but once pressure is achieved, you will want to maintain pressure. So when pressure has been achieved, drop the burner back to medium for the duration of the cooking time.

Some recipes say: "When pressure is released naturally." Those recipes need that time to complete the cooking process. Please follow the instructions for the best texture and flavor. I've tested and perfected these tried and true recipes, but if you need further assistance, feel free to leave a message for me through my website, www.debramurraycooking.com.

Pressure Cooker Tips

Here is a list of tips to help you get the most from your pressure cooker:

* It is very important to have a liquid, such as water, stock, juice, or wine, in the pressure cooker in order to create steam. Thicker sauces, such as barbecue or tomato sauce, will not create steam. At least 1 to 2 cups are necessary to create adequate steam.

* When cooking a rice, bean, or pasta dish, do not fill the pressure cooker more than halfway. When cooking soup or stocks, do not exceed the ⅔ mark.

* You should carefully wash the lid and remove the regulator for cleaning. The valves and regulator need to be cleaned for the pressure cooker to operate properly. Remove the gasket, hand wash, and properly fit back on the lid, as it prevents the steam from escaping. If it is not properly installed, steam will escape under the lid and pressure will not be achieved.

* I do not recommend using the quick-release method for letting out pressure unless the recipe calls for adding additional ingredients. Some recipes—like rice, for instance—need the extra time from allowing pressure to slowly release on its own to absorb and finish the cooking process. Also, remember never to attempt to open the lid while pressure-cooking is in progress. Wait until the pressure is fully vented before opening the lid.

* If you live in higher altitudes, you may need to increase the cooking times slightly. I suggest extending the cooking time by 5 percent for every 1,000 feet above sea level.

* All the recipes were tested by weight, so if you wish to cook a larger piece of meat, you will need to increase the cooking time. Add 10 minutes to the suggested cooking time for every additional pound of meat.

* If your meat is not as tender as you would like it, simply add ½ cup of liquid and increase the cook time by 10 minutes.

* If you ever complete a recipe and the cooking liquid is thinner than you would like, simply reduce with the lid off until the desired consistency is achieved.

Soups and Stews

Southwest Beef Vegetable Soup

Who doesn't adore this soup!? It's like a taco in a spoon—yummy and nutritious! A great game day treat.

Serves 6 to 8

1 tablespoon extra-virgin olive oil

1 pounds beef stew meat, cut into 1-inch pieces

1 teaspoon kosher salt

¼ teaspoon ground black pepper

½ teaspoon ground cumin

1 beef bone with marrow (optional)

1 medium onion, chopped

2 celery stalks, chopped

3 carrots, peeled and chopped

1 cup corn

1 cup cooked black beans

4 cups beef stock

1 green Serrano chili, seeded and chopped

2 tablespoons Worcestershire sauce

2 tablespoons chopped fresh cilantro

One 16-ounce can petite diced tomatoes

½ cup crumbled corn tortillas

Chopped green onions and lime wedges for garnish

1 Preheat the pressure cooker for 2 minutes, add the oil, and heat for an additional 2 minutes.

2 Season the beef stew meat with the kosher salt, pepper and cumin.

3 Place the beef chunks and the bone into the pressure cooker and brown for 3 minutes on each side.

4 Add the onion, celery, and carrots and cook for 5 minutes longer.

5 Add the corn, black beans, stock, chili, Worcestershire sauce, cilantro, and tomatoes to the pressure cooker; secure the lid.

6 When pressure is achieved, set a timer for 30 minutes.

7 When the cook time is complete and pressure is fully released, remove the lid with caution.

8 Stir in the tortillas, top with green onions and lime wedges, and serve.

Lamb and Vegetable Soup

You don't need to wait for St. Patrick's Day to prepare this simple but hearty lamb stew. Your family will love it any day of the year.

Serves 4

2 teaspoons extra-virgin olive oil

1 pound lamb shoulder, cut into ¾-inch cubes

14 ounces beef stock

1¼ cups dry red wine

2 garlic cloves, minced

1 sprig fresh thyme

1 bay leaf

2 cups peeled and diced butternut squash

1 cup peeled and diced parsnips

1 cup peeled and diced sweet potato

1 cup diced celery

1 medium onion, diced

½ cup Greek-style yogurt

3 tablespoons all-purpose flour

1   Heat the oil in the pressure cooker and brown the lamb in batches; drain the fat.

2   Add the stock, wine, garlic, thyme, and bay leaf to the pressure cooker; secure the lid.

3   When pressure is achieved, set a timer for 25 minutes.

4   When the cook time is complete and pressure is fully released, remove the lid with caution.

5   Add the squash, parsnips, sweet potato, celery, and onion; secure lid.

6   When the pressure is achieved, set a timer for 5 minutes.

7   When the cook time is complete and pressure is fully released, remove the lid with caution.

8   Remove and discard the thyme and bay leaf.

9   In a small mixing bowl, combine the yogurt and flour. Stir in ½ cup hot liquid from the stew into the yogurt mixture.

10 Pour the mixture into the pressure cooker and, with the lid off, stir until thickened.

11 Serve immediately.

Lentils with Italian Sausage

This delicious soup is so hearty that it is a meal on its own.
I substitute turkey sausage to lighten it up on occasion.

Serves 4

1 pound sweet Italian sausage,
cut into 1-inch pieces

1 medium onion, diced

2 garlic cloves, sliced

1 large carrot, peeled and thinly
sliced

1 celery stalk, thinly sliced

1 cup lentils

2 cups chicken stock

One 14.5-ounce can diced
tomatoes with garlic and olive oil

1 bay leaf

½ teaspoon crushed red pepper
flakes (optional)

1   Place all of the ingredients into the pressure cooker;
    secure the lid.

2   When pressure is achieved, set a timer for 20 minutes.

3   When the cook time is complete and pressure is fully
    released, remove the lid with caution.

4   Remove and discard the bay leaf and serve
    immediately.

Creamy Cauliflower Soup

Low in calories and fat, but high in vitamin C,
the cauliflower in this creamy soup will fill you up
on a winter day and help you fight against colds.

Serves 6

2 large heads cauliflower,
stem and leaves removed

1 medium sweet onion, chopped

3 garlic cloves, minced

½ teaspoon kosher salt

¼ teaspoon freshly ground
black pepper

4 cups chicken stock

¼ cup white wine

1 sprig fresh thyme

1 cup heavy cream

¼ cup shredded Cheddar cheese

Chopped fresh chives for garnish

1 Place the cauliflower, onion, garlic, kosher salt, pepper, and stock into the pressure cooker.

2 Pour in the wine and sprig of fresh thyme.

3 Secure the pressure cooker lid.

4 When pressure is achieved, set a timer for 10 minutes.

5 When the cook time is complete and pressure is fully released, remove the lid with caution.

6 Remove and discard the thyme.

7 Scoop out half the cauliflower and transfer to the carafe of a blender, along with the cream and cheese.

8 Process until smooth.

9 Pour the blender contents back into the pressure cooker and stir.

10 Garnish with the chives and serve immediately.

Tortilla Soup

The cilantro is what makes this dish so flavorful. Start your fiesta with Tortilla Soup, or eat it as your main course. This soup tastes great alongside a taco salad or before beef enchiladas.

Serves 6

2 ears fresh corn, husked

4 garlic cloves, sliced

1 large onion, diced

2 teaspoons ground cumin

Two 10-ounce cans diced tomatoes and green chilis

12 corn tortilla chips, plus more for serving

1 boneless, skinless chicken breast, diced

6 cups chicken stock

1 cup refried beans

2 tablespoons chopped fresh cilantro, for serving

1 teaspoon Parmesan cheese, for serving

1 Cut the corn kernels off the cob using a sharp knife and place the cobs and kernels in the pressure cooker.

2 Add the garlic, onion, cumin, tomatoes, tortilla chips, chicken, and stock to the pressure cooker; secure the lid.

3 When pressure is achieved, set a timer for 25 minutes.

4 When the cook time is complete and pressure is fully released, remove the lid with caution.

5 Discard the corncobs and stir in the refried beans.

6 Top with the cilantro and Parmesan cheese and serve with more corn tortilla chips, if desired.

Bursting with Beans Soup

Beans, beans, beans... a great family favorite. There is nothing better than having a hot pot of bean soup ready in minutes after a long day. Fill your favorite oversize mug and add some cornbread, and you can cozy up on the couch with this easy dinner.

Serves 4 to 6

1 pound fifteen-bean soup mix

1 large onion, diced

One 28-ounce can crushed tomatoes

3 celery stalks, chopped

1 ham hock

1 pound pork shoulder, diced into 1-inch cubes

2 garlic cloves, minced

1 tablespoon chopped fresh parsley

1 bay leaf

1 teaspoon dried rosemary

2 teaspoons kosher salt

1 teaspoon freshly ground black pepper

8 cups chicken stock

1   Place all of the ingredients into the pressure cooker; secure the lid.

2   When pressure is achieved, set a timer for 30 minutes.

3   When the cook time is complete and pressure is fully released, remove the lid with caution.

4   Remove and discard the ham hock and bay leaf.

Beef Bourguignon

Beef Bourguignon is a hearty dish for any season. Serve with buttered noodles or mashed potatoes to satisfy bigger appetites. Buttered, crusty, and warm bread always adds to this meal.

Serves 4 to 6

1 tablespoon all-purpose flour

1 teaspoon kosher salt

½ teaspoon freshly ground black pepper

1½ pounds sirloin, cut into 1-inch pieces

2 garlic cloves, minced

1 cup Burgundy wine

1½ cups beef stock

1 tablespoon tomato paste

1 sprig fresh thyme

1 cup frozen pearl onions

1 cup small mushrooms

3 carrots, peeled and sliced diagonally into 2-inch pieces

3 parsnips, peeled and cut into 2-inch pieces

1   In a bowl, combine the flour, kosher salt, and pepper; mix well.

2   Roll the beef pieces in the flour mixture; shake off excess.

3   Place the beef, garlic, wine, stock, tomato paste, thyme, onions, mushrooms, carrots, and parsnips into the pressure cooker; secure the lid.

4   When pressure is achieved, set a timer for 20 minutes.

5   When the cook time is complete and pressure is fully released, remove the lid with caution.

6   Remove and discard the thyme and serve immediately.

Butternut Squash Soup

I love to serve this soup in a demitasse. Top it with a dab of crème fraîche and serve it as the first course of a dinner party!

Serves 4

6 cups peeled and diced butternut squash

3 cups chicken stock

1 cup apple cider

2 medium apples, peeled and seeded

2 teaspoons curry powder

1 medium onion, diced

½ teaspoon kosher salt

¼ teaspoon ground nutmeg

Sprinkle of pumpkin seeds or sage for garnish, if desired

1 Place all of the ingredients into the pressure cooker; secure the lid.

2 When pressure is achieved, set a timer for 10 minutes.

3 When the cook time is complete and pressure is fully released, remove the lid with caution.

4 Purée the soup in a blender, garnish, and serve.

Chicken Soup

Not only will this delicious soup soothe the soul, but the high amount of collagen in the broth will be great for the body too!

Serves 4

1 whole chicken (about 4 pounds)

1 medium onion, quartered

6 cups water

1 tablespoon kosher salt

6 whole black peppercorns

2 celery stalks, diced

2 carrots, peeled and sliced

1 parsnip, peeled and sliced

1 sprig fresh rosemary

1 sprig fresh thyme

1 tablespoon chopped fresh parsley

1   Place the chicken, onion, water, kosher salt, and peppercorns into the pressure cooker; secure the lid.

2   When pressure is achieved, set a timer for 45 minutes.

3   When the cook time is complete and pressure is fully released, remove the lid with caution.

4   Strain the stock, and set aside.

5   Remove the chicken meat from the bones and place the meat back into the pressure cooker.

6   Add the strained stock, celery, carrots, parsnips, rosemary, and thyme to the pressure cooker; secure lid.

7   When pressure is achieved, set a timer for 5 minutes.

8   When the cook time is complete and pressure is fully released, remove the lid with caution.

9   Remove and discard the rosemary and thyme.

10 Sprinkle the soup with parsley and serve.

Chili Verde

Mild to medium, this green chili will warm your taste buds. The tomatillos add not only their flavor, but also the green color. Top this Chili Verde off with some tortilla chips and lime wedges.

Serves 4 to 6

2 pounds boneless pork loin, cut into 2-inch cubes

1 cup chicken stock

One 4-ounce can green chilis, chopped

4 tomatillos, husks removed, chopped

1 tablespoon fresh lime juice

1 teaspoon kosher salt

½ teaspoon freshly ground black pepper

1 teaspoon cumin seeds

1 teaspoon ground coriander

2 garlic cloves, minced

1 small onion, chopped

3 tablespoons chopped fresh cilantro

Sour cream for garnish

1 Place the pork, stock, green chilis, tomatillos, lime juice, kosher salt, pepper, cumin, coriander, garlic, and onion into the pressure cooker; secure the lid.

2 When pressure is achieved, set a timer for 40 minutes.

3 When the cook time is complete and pressure is fully released, remove the lid with caution.

4 Sprinkle with cilantro.

5 Serve in bowls topped with sour cream.

Fish Stock

I like to use a small amount of this stock anytime I am preparing a fish or seafood dish. To make this fast and super easy, I pour the stock into ice cube trays and freeze. Once frozen, the cubes can be stored in a freezer bag for up to 6 months.

Makes 4 cups

2 pounds fish heads from white fish, such as snapper or grouper

1 medium onion, quartered

1 celery stalk

1 carrot

2 sprigs fresh thyme

6 whole black peppercorns

½ teaspoon kosher salt

4 cups water

1 Place all of the ingredients into the pressure cooker; secure the lid.

2 When pressure is achieved, set a timer for 25 minutes.

3 When the cook time is complete and pressure is fully released, remove the lid with caution.

4 Strain using a cheesecloth-lined colander or sieve.

5 Cover and refrigerate for up to 7 days.

French Onion Soup

Whether as an appetizer or a main course, French Onion Soup is a crowd pleaser. It's the perfect appetizer to start off a steak dinner. When eating it as a main course, just add a green salad and a crispy baguette.

Serves 4 to 6

4 large sweet onions, sliced

2 cups beef stock

1 tablespoon balsamic vinegar

¼ cup red wine

2 sprigs fresh thyme

1 bay leaf

½ teaspoon kosher salt

½ teaspoon freshly ground black pepper

8 ounces Gruyère cheese, sliced

6 crostini, optional

1 Place the onions, stock, vinegar, wine, thyme, bay leaf, kosher salt, and pepper into the pressure cooker; secure the lid.

2 When pressure is achieved, set a timer for 20 minutes.

3 When the cook time is complete and pressure is fully released, remove the lid with caution.

4 Remove and discard the thyme and bay leaf.

5 Turn the oven on to broil.

6 Ladle the soup into ovenproof bowls, and top each one with 2 slices of the cheese.

7 Place the bowls under the broiler for two minutes, or until the cheese is melted.

8 Serve immediately, with crostini on the side if desired.

20 min.

Avgolemono Soup

This classic Greek dish is a creamy soup that doesn't use cream. The eggs are the secret to the soup's silky texture! Dip your favorite bread and savor the flavor.

Serves 4 to 6

6 cups chicken stock

2 boneless, skinless chicken breasts

1 teaspoon freshly ground black pepper

1 teaspoon turmeric powder

1 teaspoon kosher salt

1 bay leaf

1 teaspoon lemon zest

1 medium onion, chopped

1 celery stalk, sliced

1 carrot, peeled and sliced

¼ cup dry orzo, rinsed

½ cup fresh lemon juice

2 large eggs, beaten

1 egg yolk, beaten

3 fresh mint leaves, chopped

1 Place the stock, chicken breasts, pepper, turmeric, kosher salt, bay leaf, lemon zest, onion, celery, and carrot into the pressure cooker; secure the lid.

2 When pressure is achieved, set a timer for 20 minutes.

3 When the cook time is complete and pressure is fully released, remove the lid with caution.

4 Pour the pressure cooker contents through a strainer, separating the stock from the chicken and vegetables.

5 Pour the stock back into the pressure cooker.

6 Discard all of the vegetables and chop the chicken; set aside.

7 Turn pressure on and cook with the lid off for 3 minutes.

8 Stir in the orzo and cook for 5 more minutes.

9 When cooking is complete, combine the lemon juice, eggs, and yolk in a bowl; whisk well.

10 Ladle ¼ cup of hot stock into the egg mixture; whisk well.

11 Drizzle the egg mixture into the pressure cooker while continuously whisking.

12 Add the chicken and mint to the pressure cooker.

13 Cook for an additional 3 minutes before serving.

14 Serve immediately.

Barley Beef Soup

A satisfying one-dish meal that will delight you and your family. Reheat the leftovers for a filling lunch on a cold winter's day to warm your soul.

Serves 4 to 6

1 tablespoon extra-virgin olive oil

¾ pound beef chuck, cut into 1-inch cubes

1 teaspoon kosher salt

½ teaspoon freshly ground black pepper

4 cups beef stock

One 14.5-ounce can crushed tomatoes

1 cup chopped onion

½ cup chopped celery

2 garlic cloves, minced

1 teaspoon dried oregano

¼ teaspoon red pepper flakes

1 bay leaf

1 cup peeled and diced potatoes

¼ cup dry quick-cooking barley

1 cup frozen mixed vegetables

1 Heat the oil in the pressure cooker, add the meat, sprinkle with kosher salt and pepper, and cook until browned; drain the fat.

2 Stir in the stock, scraping up all the little bits from the bottom of the pan.

3 Add the tomatoes, onion, celery, garlic, oregano, red pepper flakes, and bay leaf to the pressure cooker; secure the lid.

4 When pressure is achieved, set a timer for 25 minutes.

5 When the cook time is complete and pressure is fully released, remove the lid with caution.

6 Add the barley and mixed vegetables; secure lid.

7 When pressure is achieved, set the timer for 5 minutes.

8 When the cook time is complete and pressure is fully released, remove the lid with caution.

9 Remove and discard the bay leaf and serve.

Ginger-Carrot Soup

This Ginger-Carrot Soup is creamy, smooth, and nourishing. Want some crunch? Add a handful of toasted pumpkin or sunflower seeds. And for the little ones, add a grilled peanut butter sandwich—they won't say no.

Serves 4 to 6

6 carrots, peeled and chopped

1 medium onion, diced

2 tablespoons minced fresh ginger

2 cups chicken stock

½ cup orange juice

1 teaspoon kosher salt

½ teaspoon freshly ground black pepper

1 Place all of the ingredients into the pressure cooker; secure the lid.

2 When pressure is achieved, set a timer for 5 minutes.

3 When the cook time is complete and pressure is fully released, remove the lid with caution.

4 Purée the soup in a blender and serve.

Beef Stock

This flavorful stock will enhance any recipe that requires beef stock. Homemade beef stock beats the canned versions by far. This Beef Stock recipe is particularly great as a base for my French Onion Soup (page 24).

Makes 5 cups

2 pounds beef ribs

1 tablespoon extra-virgin olive oil

2 teaspoon kosher salt, divided

1 teaspoon ground pepper, divided

1 large onion, quartered

2 Roma tomatoes, halved

1 turnip, halved

2 carrots, peeled

1 sprig fresh thyme

1 sprig fresh rosemary

1 bay leaf

4 cups water

1 cup dry red wine

1 Preheat oven to 400°F.

2 Rub the ribs with oil and half the kosher salt and ground pepper, and place them on a roasting pan.

3 Place the pan in the oven and let roast for 25 minutes.

4 When roasting is complete, transfer the ribs to the pressure cooker.

5 Add onion, water, and the remaining kosher salt and ground pepper to the pressure cooker; secure the lid.

6 When pressure is achieved, set a timer for 35 minutes.

7 When the cook time is complete and pressure is fully released, remove the lid with caution.

8 Add the carrots, thyme, rosemary, bay leaf, water, and wine; secure lid.

9 When pressure is achieved, set a timer for 15 minutes.

10 When the cook time is complete and pressure is fully released, remove the lid with caution.

11 Strain with a sieve and refrigerate the stock for 5 hours; remove the fat.

12 Cover and refrigerate up to 5 days.

Rice Noodle Soup with Shrimp

For a true Asian taste made easy, try Rice Noodle Soup with Shrimp. The grated ginger and chili give a little kick to this delicious meal.

Serves 4 to 6

5 cups chicken stock

4 garlic cloves, sliced

1 tablespoon fresh ginger, grated

1 star anise

3 tablespoons fish sauce

1 tablespoon soy sauce

1 teaspoon brown sugar

1 Serrano chili, seeds and membrane removed, thinly sliced

1 lemongrass stalk, halved

1 teaspoon lime zest

1 pound large shrimp, peeled and deveined

2 cups bean sprouts

2 scallions, cut into 1-inch pieces

2 tablespoons chopped fresh cilantro

1 lime, cut into wedges

2 tablespoons chopped fresh mint

6 ounces dry rice noodles, cooked

1   Place the stock, garlic, ginger, star anise, fish sauce, soy sauce, brown sugar, Serrano, lemongrass, and lime zest into the pressure cooker; secure the lid.

2   When pressure is achieved, set a timer for 15 minutes.

3   When the cook time is complete and pressure is fully released, remove the lid with caution.

4   Remove the lemongrass and then add the shrimp, bean sprouts, scallions, cilantro, lime, and rice noodles to the pressure cooker; stir.

5   Divide the soup between bowls and serve.

Cream of Root Vegetable Soup

A tummy-warmer for that chilly, fall day, this soup is all about the vegetables, with a creamy base. You'll want to make an extra batch, because you'll be craving more.

Serves 6

6 cups chicken stock

2 celery stalks, chopped

1 leek, white part only, sliced

2 Yukon Gold potatoes, diced

1 turnip, peeled and diced

2 parsnips, peeled and diced

1 celery root, peeled and diced

1 teaspoon kosher salt

½ teaspoon white pepper

¼ teaspoon ground coriander

2 tablespoons heavy cream

1 tablespoon unsalted butter

Chopped fresh chives and parsley for garnish

1 Place the stock, celery, leek, potatoes, turnip, parsnips, celery root, kosher salt, pepper, and coriander into the pressure cooker; secure the lid.

2 When pressure is achieved, set a timer for 25 minutes.

3 When the cook time is complete and pressure is fully released, remove the lid with caution.

4 When the soup has cooled slightly, add the cream and unsalted butter. Using an immersion blender, purée the soup until smooth.

5 Garnish the soup with the chives and parsley and serve immediately.

Italian Cabbage Soup

Brimming with fresh vegetables, Italian Cabbage Soup will become a staple, as all of the ingredients are easy to find. Garnish with a sprinkle of Parmesan cheese and serve with warm buttered rolls.

Serves 6 to 8

2 medium onions, sliced

1 red bell pepper, chopped

1 head cabbage, sliced

1 parsnip, peeled and diced

4 celery stalks, cut into 1-inch pieces

1 sprig fresh rosemary

1 sprig fresh thyme

2 garlic cloves, minced

4 cups beef stock

One 28-ounce can diced tomatoes

1 teaspoon kosher salt

½ teaspoon freshly ground black pepper

1 tablespoon balsamic vinegar

½ teaspoon coriander seeds

1 bay leaf

1 pound hot Italian sausage, cooked and drained of fat

1 Place all of the ingredients into the pressure cooker; secure the lid.

2 When pressure is achieved, set a timer for 30 minutes.

3 When the cook time is complete and pressure is fully released, remove the lid with caution.

4 Remove and discard the rosemary, thyme, and bay leaf and serve immediately.

Kabocha Squash Soup

Kabocha squash has a naturally sweet flavor and is an excellent source of beta carotene, which can be converted to vitamin A. Kabocha is also a good source of fiber. Garnish this soup with sour cream and cranberry sauce.

Serves 4 to 6

1 Kabocha squash (about 2½ pounds), peeled, seeded, and cut into 2-inch pieces

2 cups chicken stock

1 small onion, chopped

3 garlic cloves, sliced

1 teaspoons kosher salt

1 teaspoon freshly ground black pepper

2 tablespoons fresh ginger, peeled and sliced

¼ cup orange juice

1 tablespoon brown sugar

1 Place all of the ingredients into the pressure cooker; secure the lid.

2 When pressure is achieved, set a timer for 10 minutes.

3 When the cook time is complete and pressure is fully released, remove the lid with caution.

4 Using an immersion blender, purée the soup until it is smooth and serve.

10 min.

Lobster Asparagus Soup

This is a beautiful, rich soup, and it's delicious hot or cold. For a fun entertaining idea, serve it in a shot glass topped with a piece of lobster. Your guests will be super impressed.

Serves 4

2 cups chicken stock

1 cup white wine

1 lemon, halved

1 leek, white part only, sliced

1 celery stalk, thinly sliced

2 lobster tails, with shells

1 teaspoon lemon pepper seasoning

1 pound fresh asparagus, cut into 1-inch pieces

4 ounces cream cheese

1   Place the stock, wine, lemon, leek, celery, lobster, lemon pepper, and asparagus into the pressure cooker; secure the lid.

2   When pressure is achieved, set a timer for 10 minutes.

3   When the cook time is complete and pressure is fully released, remove the lid with caution.

4   Remove the lobster meat from the tails and discard the shells.

5   Cut the lobster meat into ½-inch pieces and place them back into the pressure cooker.

6   Add the cream cheese to the pressure cooker and stir until dissolved.

7   Serve hot or cold.

15 min.

Tuscan Meatball Soup

A time-tested favorite full of hearty home-style meatballs, this flavorful dish will satisfy as a Sunday dinner get-together or a weekday meal. Feel free to substitute with frozen store-bought meatballs.

Serves 6 to 8

MEATBALLS

1 pound lean ground beef or turkey

1 small onion, minced

¾ cup Italian bread crumbs with Romano cheese

1 teaspoon garlic kosher salt

1 large egg, beaten

SOUP

4 cups chicken stock

½ cup peeled and sliced carrot

2 celery stalks, thinly sliced

1 small onion, diced

1 bay leaf

One 14.5-ounce can diced tomatoes

One 19-ounce can great Northern beans

1 cup dry orecchiette

1 teaspoon garlic kosher salt

FOR THE MEATBALLS:

1   In a bowl, combine all of the ingredients; mix well.

2   Form the mixture into 1-inch meatballs.

FOR THE SOUP:

1   Place the meatballs and all of the soup ingredients into the pressure cooker; secure the lid.

2   When pressure has been achieved, set a timer for 15 minutes.

3   When the cook time is complete and pressure is fully released, remove the lid with caution.

4   Remove and discard the bay leaf and serve immediately.

Old-Fashioned Beef Stew

This delicious stew is so fast and easy in your pressure cooker, any night can now be stew night. Wait until you taste how delicious the carrots are in this dish!

Serves 6 to 8

2 pounds beef stew meat, cut into 1-inch cubes

1 cup beef stock

1 medium onion, diced

2 sprigs fresh thyme

1 teaspoon kosher salt

½ teaspoon freshly ground black pepper

3 tablespoons tomato paste

1 tablespoon grape jelly

1 pound small red potatoes, peeled and quartered

2 celery stalks, cut into 1-inch pieces

2 carrots, peeled and cut into 1-inch pieces

1 Place the stew meat, stock, onion, thyme, kosher salt, pepper, tomato paste, and jelly into the pressure cooker; secure the lid.

2 When pressure is achieved, set a timer for 20 minutes.

3 When the cook time is complete and pressure is fully released, remove the lid with caution.

4 Add the potatoes, celery, and carrots to the pressure cooker; secure lid.

5 When pressure is achieved, set a timer for 5 minutes.

6 When the cook time is complete and pressure is fully released, remove the lid with caution.

7 Remove and discard the thyme and serve.

Pizza Soup

Pizza isn't just for college kids. This smart recipe
is packed with my favorite Italian ingredients. Serve
Pizza Soup with a side of garlic knots for dipping,
or make it ahead of time and keep warm for a family
on the go.

Serves 4 to 6

One 28-ounce can petite diced
tomatoes

1 medium onion, chopped

4 garlic cloves, sliced

1 teaspoon kosher salt

1 teaspoon freshly ground
black pepper

1 teaspoon dried oregano

1 pound hot Italian sausage,
thinly sliced

3 ounces pepperoni, diced

1 green bell pepper, diced

½ cup dry ditalini pasta

½ cup shredded mozzarella
cheese for serving

1   Place the tomatoes, onion, garlic, kosher salt, pepper,
    oregano, sausage, pepperoni, pepper, and pasta into
    the pressure cooker; secure the lid.

2   When pressure is achieved, set a timer for 8 minutes.

3   When the cook time is complete and pressure is fully
    released, remove the lid with caution.

4   Divide the soup among bowls, top with the cheese,
    and serve.

Rich Chicken Stock

This Rich Chicken Stock is great for the soups and other recipes included in this book. Use this homemade stock instead of water when cooking rice in a pressure cooker for full-on flavor.

Makes 5 cups

3 pounds chicken wings

1 medium onion, quartered

1 carrot, peeled

1 celery stalk

1 parsnip, peeled

1 sprig fresh thyme

1 sprig fresh rosemary

1 tablespoon extra-virgin olive oil

3 teaspoons kosher salt, divided

1 teaspoon freshly ground black pepper

5 cups water

5 whole black peppercorns

1   Preheat the oven to 400°F.

2   Place the chicken wings, onion, carrot, celery, parsnip, thyme, and rosemary on a roasting pan. Drizzle with olive oil and sprinkle with 2 teaspoons of the kosher salt and the ground pepper.

3   Place the pan in the oven and roast for 40 minutes.

4   When roasting is complete, drain the fat and place the contents of the pan into the pressure cooker.

5   Add the water, the remaining 1 teaspoon kosher salt, and the peppercorns to the pressure cooker; secure the lid.

6   When pressure is achieved, set a timer for 45 minutes.

7   When the cook time is complete and pressure is fully released, remove the lid with caution.

8   Strain using a colander.

9   Refrigerate the stock for 5 hours, and remove the hardened fat before using.

Potato-Leek Soup

When served piping hot, a sprinkle of Cheddar cheese and bacon bits makes this dish extra rich and savory. Refrigerate overnight, and this soup is even more delicious served cold!

Serves 4 to 6

2 cups sliced leeks, white part only

1 cup sliced sweet onion

2 cups peeled and diced Yukon Gold potatoes

3 cups chicken stock

½ teaspoon kosher salt

½ teaspoon freshly ground black pepper

½ cup sour cream for serving

1 teaspoon chopped fresh chives for serving

1   Place the leeks, onion, potatoes, stock, kosher salt, and pepper into the pressure cooker; secure the lid.

2   When pressure is achieved, set a timer for 10 minutes.

3   When the cook time is complete and pressure is fully released, remove the lid with caution.

4   Using an immersion blender, purée the soup until it reaches the desired consistency.

5   Serve topped with the sour cream and chives.

Shrimp Bisque

Hard to resist, soup doesn't get any better than this creamy bisque. Feel free to change up the heat in this recipe to your liking. I suggest sweet paprika, but if you're feeling spicy, go bold and substitute cayenne pepper.

Serves 4 to 8

2 pounds large shrimp, with shells

1 teaspoon kosher salt

1 teaspoon freshly ground black pepper

1 teaspoon sweet paprika

1 cup white wine

3 cups chicken stock

1 carrot, peeled and chopped

1 celery stalk, chopped

1 leek (white part only), sliced

1 garlic clove, sliced

1 small potato, peeled and halved

1 tablespoon tomato paste

1 sprig fresh tarragon

2 teaspoons sherry

1 cup heavy cream

1   Peel and devein the shrimp, removing the tails. Place the shrimp shells and tails in the pressure cooker.

2   Season the shells with the kosher salt and pepper. Add the wine and stock to the pressure cooker; secure the lid.

3   When pressure is achieved, set a timer for 6 minutes.

4   When the cook time is complete and pressure is fully released, remove the lid with caution.

5   Strain the stock through a sieve.

6   Add the shrimp, carrot, celery, leek, garlic, potato, tomato paste, tarragon, and sherry to the pressure cooker; secure the lid.

7   When pressure is achieved, set the timer for 6 minutes.

8   When the cook time is complete and pressure is fully released, remove the lid with caution.

9   Remove and discard the tarragon.

10 Using an immersion blender, purée the soup while adding the cream. Purée until its reaches the desired consistency and serve.

10 min.

Swiss Chard and White Bean Stew

Talk about healthy! This dish is rich in vitamins K, A, and C and is filled with nutrients. This yummy soup will more than heal the soul. Top it with grated Parmesan cheese and serve with a slice of crusty bread.

Serves 4 to 6

1 bunch Swiss chard, ribs removed and chopped

1 medium sweet onion, diced

3 garlic cloves, sliced

1 pound red bliss potatoes, diced

1 cup canned white beans

2 sprigs fresh thyme

1 cup vegetable stock

1 teaspoon kosher salt

½ teaspoon freshly ground black pepper

1   Place all of the ingredients into the pressure cooker; secure the lid.

2   When pressure is achieved, set a timer for 10 minutes.

3   When the cook time is complete and pressure is fully released, remove the lid with caution.

4   Remove and discard the thyme and serve.

Split Pea Soup

You can't go wrong with this meaty split pea soup. Typically simmered for hours, this dish will be bursting with flavor in 10 minutes when cooked in the pressure cooker. Pair this hearty Split Pea Soup with flaky biscuits and unsalted butter.

Serves 6 to 8

1 package (16 ounces) split peas with seasoning packet

2 cups diced pork shoulder

3 carrots, peeled and sliced

½ cup diced onion

2 celery stalks, sliced

2 garlic cloves, minced

1 bay leaf

2 tablespoons chopped fresh parsley

1 tablespoon kosher salt

½ teaspoon freshly ground black pepper

1 teaspoon apple cider vinegar

6 cups water

1   Place all of the ingredients into the pressure cooker; secure the lid.

2   When pressure is achieved, set a timer for 10 minutes.

3   When the cook time is complete and pressure is fully released, remove the lid with caution.

4   Remove and discard the bay leaf and serve.

Texas-Style Chili

You don't have to be a cowboy to try this heartier version of traditional chili. My Texas-Style Chili packs heat behind savory chunks of beef sirloin and pork loin. I like to serve it in hollowed-out corn muffins for a fun and entertaining presentation.

Serves 6 to 8

2 pounds beef sirloin, cut into 1-inch pieces

1 pound pork loin, cut into 1-inch pieces

1 bell pepper, diced

1 medium onion, diced

3 garlic cloves, minced

2 teaspoons chili powder

2 whole chipotles in adobo sauce, chopped fine

1 teaspoon ground cumin

1 teaspoon kosher salt

½ teaspoon freshly ground black pepper

2 cups beef stock

One 15-ounce can dark red kidney beans

One 28-ounce can diced tomatoes

One 10-ounce can tomatoes with green chilis and lime

2 tablespoons tomato paste

1   Place the beef, pork, bell pepper, onion, garlic, chili powder, chipotles, cumin, kosher salt, pepper, and stock into the pressure cooker; secure the lid.

2   When pressure is achieved, set a timer for 30 minutes.

3   When the cook time is complete and pressure is fully released, remove the lid with caution.

4   Add the kidney beans, diced tomatoes, tomatoes with chilis and lime, and tomato paste to the pressure cooker; secure the lid.

5   When pressure is achieved, set a timer for 10 minutes.

6   When the cook time is complete and pressure is fully released, remove the lid with caution.

7   Serve immediately.

Tomato Florentine

Dip your grilled cheese into this tomato soup for an adult version of a childhood favorite. For extra flavor, garnish with a touch of pesto.

Serves 4 to 6

2 pounds grape tomatoes

6 cups chicken stock

1 carrot, peeled and sliced

1 medium onion, chopped

3 garlic cloves, sliced

1 teaspoon kosher salt

1 teaspoon freshly ground black pepper

1 cup dry small shells pasta

1 cup baby spinach leaves

5 fresh basil leaves, torn, for serving

1   Place the grape tomatoes, stock, carrot, onion, garlic, kosher salt, pepper, pasta, and baby spinach into the pressure cooker; secure the lid.

2   When pressure is achieved, set a timer for 8 minutes.

3   When the cook time is complete and pressure is fully released, remove the lid with caution.

4   Top with basil leaves and serve.

Classic Tomato Soup

This staple works best with a grilled cheese. To put a twist on this family favorite, opt for an aged Gruyère between sourdough bread slices. If you're watching your gluten intake, try baking freshly grated Parmesan cheese to create tuiles for a guilt-free topping.

Serves 4 to 6

4 pints grape tomatoes

2 cups chicken stock

2 sprigs fresh thyme

1 small onion, quartered

2 carrots, peeled and thinly sliced

2 celery stalks, thinly sliced

1 small potato, peeled and halved

2 teaspoons kosher salt

1 teaspoon freshly ground black pepper

2 tablespoons unsalted butter

Fresh basil leaves for garnish

1   Place the tomatoes, stock, and thyme into the pressure cooker; secure the lid.

2   When pressure is achieved, set a timer for 20 minutes.

3   When the cook time is complete and pressure is fully released, remove the lid with caution.

4   Remove and discard the thyme, and press the tomatoes through a sieve to remove the seeds and skin.

5   Add the strained tomato liquid, onion, carrots, celery, potato, kosher salt, and pepper to the pressure cooker; secure the lid.

6   When pressure is achieved, set a timer for 10 minutes.

7   When the cook time is complete and pressure is fully released, remove the lid with caution.

8   Transfer the soup to the carafe of a blender, along with the unsalted butter.

9   Process until the soup reaches the desired consistency.

10   Serve garnished with basil leaves.

Vegetable Stock

This flavorful, nutrient-rich stock is perfect stored in ice cube trays so you can use a splash any time you want to pop some flavor into your favorite vegetable or meat dish.

Makes 5 cups

4 medium onions, quartered skin on

4 medium carrots, peeled and cut into 2-inch pieces

3 medium potatoes, halved

2 parsnips, peeled and cut into 2-inch pieces

1 small head cabbage, cut into wedges

1 tablespoon extra-virgin olive oil

½ teaspoon kosher salt

¼ teaspoon freshly ground black pepper

8 cups water

1 sprig fresh rosemary

1 sprig fresh thyme

1 tablespoon chopped fresh oregano

1   Preheat the oven to 350°F.

2   Place the onions, carrots, potatoes, parsnips, and cabbage on a roasting pan; drizzle with the olive oil, and sprinkle with the kosher salt and pepper.

3   Place the pan in the oven and let roast for 30 minutes.

4   When roasting is complete, transfer the pan ingredients along with the water, rosemary, thyme, and oregano to the pressure cooker; secure the lid.

5   When pressure is achieved, set a timer for 20 minutes.

6   When the cook time is complete and pressure is fully released, remove the lid with caution.

7   Strain the stock using a colander.

8   Cover and refrigerate the stock up to five days.

Traditional Chili

When camping with the kids, open a single-serve bag of corn chips and use it to top your bowl of chili. Add cheese and sour cream for a snack on the go with easy cleanup.

Serves 6 to 8

1½ pounds ground chuck

1 medium onion, chopped

3 garlic cloves, minced

1 Anaheim chili, seeds removed, finely chopped

1 teaspoon kosher salt

½ teaspoon ground black pepper

1 teaspoon chili powder

1 teaspoon ground cumin

1 teaspoon ground coriander

One 28-ounce can crushed tomatoes

1 cup beef stock

½ teaspoon ground cinnamon

One 15-ounce can dark red kidney beans, drained

Corn chips, shredded Cheddar cheese, chopped green onions, and sour cream for garnish

1 Place the ground chuck into the pressure cooker; cook for 5 minutes with the lid off, breaking the beef up with a wooden spoon.

2 Drain the fat and place the beef back into the pressure cooker.

3 Add the onion, garlic, chili, kosher salt, pepper, chili powder, cumin, coriander, tomatoes, stock, and cinnamon to the pressure cooker; secure the lid.

4 When pressure is achieved, set a timer for 20 minutes.

5 When the cook time is complete and pressure is fully released, remove the lid with caution.

6 Stir in the kidney beans and taste for additional seasonings.

7 Garnish with the corn chips, cheese, green onions, and sour cream.

8 Serve immediately.

White Chili

Garnish the White Chili with sour cream, shredded Cheddar cheese, and chopped green onions. To spare some calories and fat, opt for low-fat Cheddar or Greek yogurt instead of sour cream.

Serves 8

4 boneless, skinless chicken breasts

3 cups chicken stock

1 teaspoon kosher salt

½ teaspoon ground black pepper

1 teaspoon ground cumin

2 teaspoons chili powder

1 teaspoon ground coriander

1 cup minced onion

2 cloves garlic, minced

1 green jalapeño, seeds and membrane removed, diced

Two 15.5-ounce cans great Northern beans, drained

One 10.75-ounce can tomatoes with green chilis

1 tablespoon chopped fresh cilantro, divided

½ cup shredded Monterey Jack cheese

1 Place the chicken breasts, stock, salt, black pepper, cumin, chili powder, coriander, onion, and garlic into the pressure cooker; secure the lid.

2 When pressure is achieved, set a timer for 30 minutes.

3 When the cook time is complete and pressure is fully released, remove the lid with caution.

4 Add the jalapeño, beans, tomatoes and half the cilantro into the pressure cooker; secure the lid.

5 When pressure is achieved, set a timer for 5 minutes.

6 When the cook time is complete and pressure is fully released, remove the lid with caution.

7 Stir in the cheese and remaining cilantro. Serve hot.

Poultry

Chicken Cacciatore

For a complete meal cooked in 30 minutes, serve this Italian classic alongside pressure-cooked Garlic Mashed Potatoes (page 183) and Italian Green Beans (page 198). A glass of Merlot complements the juicy chicken in this romantic dinner.

Serves 6

1 whole chicken, cut into 8 pieces

¼ teaspoon Italian seasoning

1 teaspoon kosher salt

½ teaspoon freshly ground black pepper

½ teaspoon garlic powder

1 cup thinly sliced onion

1 bell pepper, thinly sliced

½ cup red wine

½ cup chicken stock

1 cup canned petite diced tomatoes

1 teaspoon capers

1   Preheat the pressure cooker add the chicken pieces to the pressure cooker skin side down to brown. You may need to do this in several batches.

2   Pour off the chicken fat from the pressure cooker.

3   Place the chicken back into the pressure cooker and season with the Italian seasoning, kosher salt, pepper, and garlic powder.

4   Add the onion, bell pepper, wine, stock, tomatoes, and capers, to the pressure cooker; secure the lid.

5   When pressure is achieved, set a timer for 20 minutes.

6   When the cook time is complete and pressure is fully released, remove the lid with caution.

7   Serve hot.

Chicken Paprika

If you like spice, feel free to opt for traditional Hungarian-style paprika for this savory chicken. Serve it on top of egg noodles or with rice.

Serves 6

4 boneless, skinless chicken breasts, cut into 2-inch pieces

1 large onion, chopped

1 teaspoon kosher salt

½ teaspoon freshly ground black pepper

1 tablespoon sweet paprika

1 cup chicken stock

One 14.5-ounce can diced tomatoes with bell peppers

1 cup heavy cream

3 garlic cloves, minced

1 tablespoon sour cream

1 tablespoon chopped fresh parsley

1   Place the chicken, onion, kosher salt, pepper, paprika, stock, tomatoes, heavy cream, and garlic into the pressure cooker; secure the lid.

2   When pressure is achieved, set a timer for 20 minutes.

3   When the cook time is complete and pressure is fully released, remove the lid with caution.

4   Stir in the sour cream, top with the parsley, and serve.

Creamy Mushroom Chicken

Mmmmm, Creamy Mushroom Chicken is perfect over your favorite pasta! So quick and easy, there's no need for takeout.

Serves 4

1 tablespoon extra-virgin olive oil

4 bone-in, skin-on chicken breasts

1 small onion, diced

1 cup sliced mushrooms

3 garlic cloves, minced

One 10.5-ounce can cream of mushroom soup

½ cup whole milk

1½ cups chicken stock

1 sprig fresh thyme

2 cups dry egg noodles

1 teaspoon kosher salt

1 teaspoon freshly ground black pepper

1 Heat the oil in a pressure cooker with the lid off, add the chicken breasts, and brown well on all sides.

2 Remove the chicken to a platter and add the onion, mushrooms and garlic to the pressure cooker, sautéing for 5 minutes.

3 Add the soup, milk, stock, thyme, and noodles, and stir.

4 Place the chicken back into the pressure cooker and add kosher salt and black pepper; secure the lid.

5 When pressure is achieved, set a timer for 10 minutes.

6 When the cook time is complete and pressure is fully released, remove the lid with caution.

7 Remove and discard the thyme and serve immediately.

Chicken Pot Pie Towers

These pot pie–filled pastries are great for luncheons. The fluffy pastry shells pull this classic together.

Serves 6

1 (10-ounce) box "tower" puff pastry shells

2 pounds bone-in, skinless chicken breasts

1 cup chicken stock

1 medium onion, halved

2 garlic cloves, minced

1 sprig fresh thyme

1 teaspoon kosher salt

½ teaspoon freshly ground black pepper

One 10.5-ounce can cream of mushroom soup

1½ cups frozen mixed vegetables

1 Prepare the puff pastry shells according to package directions.

2 Place the chicken, stock, onion, garlic, thyme, kosher salt, and pepper into the pressure cooker; secure the lid.

3 When pressure is achieved, set a timer for 20 minutes.

4 When the cook time is complete and pressure is fully released, remove the lid with caution.

5 Remove and discard the thyme, remove the chicken meat from the bones, and place the chicken meat back into the pressure cooker.

6 Add the soup and vegetables to the pressure cooker; secure lid.

7 When pressure is achieved, set a timer for 5 minutes.

8 When the cook time is complete and pressure is fully released, remove the lid with caution.

9 Place a scoop of the chicken mixture in the center of each shell and serve.

20
min.

Chicken Tacos

Perfect for Taco Tuesdays, the kids will love to make their own creation with this set-it-and-forget-it chicken. Spice it up by offering a hot sauce bar by the taco toppings.

Serves 4

3 boneless, skinless chicken breasts

1 8.8-ounce box taco dinner kit

1 cup chicken stock

1 teaspoon lime zest

1 cup shredded lettuce

1 plum tomato, diced

3 green onions, chopped

3 jalapeños, sliced

½ cup shredded Cheddar cheese

½ cup sour cream

1 Place the chicken, taco seasoning from the dinner kit, stock, and lime zest into the pressure cooker; secure the lid.

2 When pressure is achieved, set a timer for 20 minutes.

3 When the cook time is complete and pressure is fully released, remove the lid with caution.

4 Shred the chicken using two forks.

5 Arrange the chicken, along with the lettuce, tomato, green onions, jalapeños, cheese, sour cream, on the shells from the dinner kit.

6 Finish with the taco sauce and let everyone dress their tacos the way they like.

Mediterranean Chicken with Orzo

Embrace your inner Greek god or goddess when creating this scrumptious Mediterranean chicken with delicious orzo. Zeus himself would approve.

Serves 4

1 tablespoon extra-virgin olive oil

4 bone-in chicken thighs, trimmed of fat

1 teaspoon kosher salt

1 teaspoon freshly ground black pepper

1 small onion, thinly sliced

3 garlic cloves, minced

1½ cups dry orzo

1½ cups chicken stock

1 teaspoon dried oregano

1 lemon, cut into 8 wedges

½ cup Kalamata olives, pitted and chopped

1   Heat the oil in a pressure cooker with the lid off.

2   Season the chicken with kosher salt and pepper and add to the pressure cooker.

3   Brown the chicken well on both sides until the juices run clear.

4   Add the onion and garlic and continue to cook for an additional minute.

5   Add the orzo, stock, oregano, and lemon to the pressure cooker; secure the lid.

6   When pressure is achieved, set a timer for 25 minutes.

7   When the cook time is complete and pressure is fully released, remove the lid with caution.

8   Stir in the olives and serve.

Chicken and Dumplings

A go-to comfort food, this warm and cozy winter dish is perfect for those in hibernation. You know what you're having on your next snow day!

Serves 4 to 6

2 pounds boneless, skinless chicken breasts

2 cups chicken stock

1 sprig fresh thyme

1 teaspoon kosher salt

½ teaspoon freshly ground black pepper

4 carrots, peeled and sliced into 1-inch pieces

1 large onion, diced

3 celery stalks, sliced

One 10.75-ounce can cream of celery soup

One 7.5-ounce can biscuit dough, cut into squares

2 tablespoons chopped fresh parsley

1   Place the chicken, stock, thyme, kosher salt, and pepper into the pressure cooker; secure the lid.

2   When pressure is achieved, set a timer for 20 minutes.

3   When the cook time is complete and pressure is fully released, remove the lid with caution.

4   Remove and discard the thyme and add the carrots, onion, and celery to the pressure cooker; secure the lid.

5   When pressure is achieved, set a timer for 5 minutes.

6   When the cook time is complete and pressure is fully released, remove the lid with caution.

7   With the lid off, set the pressure cooker to medium heat and stir in the cream of celery soup.

8   When the liquid reaches a simmer, add the biscuit dough and cover with the lid; steam for 5 minutes.

9   When the cook time is complete, remove lid with caution. Sprinkle with the parsley and serve.

Chicken Marsala

This dish is famous for its signature flavor of Marsala wine, and the gravy is amazing drizzled over Garlic Mashed Potatoes (page 183). Add your favorite vegetable for a fast five-star meal.

Serves 4

4 boneless, skinless chicken breasts

1 cup sliced mushrooms

1 shallot, minced

½ cup chicken stock

½ cup Marsala wine

1 sprig fresh thyme

1 teaspoon kosher salt

½ teaspoon freshly ground black pepper

1 envelope brown gravy mix

1   Place all of the ingredients into the pressure cooker; secure the lid.

2   When pressure is achieved, set a timer for 12 minutes.

3   When the cook time is complete and pressure is fully released, remove the lid with caution.

4   Remove and discard the thyme and transfer the chicken to a platter; pour the sauce over the chicken and serve.

Coq au Vin

This traditional dish from Burgundy is best with chicken thighs for a braising goodness you won't get with breasts. Perfect for a cool autumn evening in front of a fire.

Serves 4 to 6

6 bone-in chicken thighs, trimmed of fat

1 tablespoon all-purpose flour

1 teaspoon kosher salt

½ teaspoon freshly ground black pepper

2 bacon strips, diced

2 tablespoons unsalted butter

8 boiler onions, peeled

1 pound whole mushrooms

2 sprigs fresh thyme

½ cup dry red wine

½ cup brandy

1 cup chicken stock

1 teaspoon sugar

1   Rub the chicken with the flour, kosher salt, and pepper.

2   Heat the pressure cooker to medium, add the bacon, and cook until crisp; remove and set aside.

3   Add the unsalted butter to the pressure cooker and let melt.

4   Add the seasoned chicken to the pressure cooker and cook until golden brown.

5   Add the onions, mushrooms, thyme, wine, brandy, stock, and sugar to the pressure cooker; secure the lid.

6   When pressure is achieved, set a timer for 40 minutes.

7   When the cook time is complete and pressure is fully released, remove the lid with caution.

8   Transfer the chicken, mushrooms, and onions to a platter, leaving the liquid in the pressure cooker.

9   With the lid off, set the pressure cooker to medium heat, and reduce the sauce for 10 minutes.

10   Remove the thyme sprigs and ladle the sauce over chicken.

11   Sprinkle with the bacon and serve.

Turkey Tacos

These tasty turkey tacos are not only flavorful, they're a healthy alternative to beef or pork. Your family will love them just as much, maybe more.

Serves 4 to 6

2 pounds boneless turkey breast

1 medium onion, chopped

4 garlic cloves, minced

2 parsnips, peeled and chopped

2 celery stalks, chopped

1 cup chicken stock

6 Roma tomatoes, diced

1 teaspoon kosher salt

½ teaspoon freshly ground black pepper

1 Serrano chili, seeded and diced

1 teaspoon ground cumin

1 bay leaf

Flour or corn tortillas for serving

1   Place all of the ingredients into the pressure cooker; secure the lid.

2   When pressure is achieved, set a timer for 30 minutes.

3   When the cook time is complete and pressure is fully released, remove the lid with caution.

4   Remove and discard the bay leaf.

5   Serve the turkey in flour or corn tortillas with all the trimmings.

Curry in a Hurry

An unintimidating ethnic dish that even your pickiest family member will love. Spice it up with this fragrant curry recipe.

Serves 4

2 pounds bone-in skinless chicken legs

1 cup chicken stock

¼ cup brown sugar

1 tablespoon curry powder

1 teaspoon garam masala

1 medium onion, chopped

1 red bell pepper, julienned

One 14.5-ounce can petite diced tomatoes

1 cup plain yogurt

1 tablespoon chopped fresh cilantro leaves

1   Place the chicken legs, stock, brown sugar, curry powder, garam masala, onion, bell pepper, and tomatoes into the pressure cooker; secure the lid.

2   When pressure is achieved, set a timer for 25 minutes.

3   When the cook time is complete and pressure is fully released, remove the lid with caution.

4   Transfer the chicken to a platter using a slotted spoon.

5   Add the yogurt to the liquid inside the pressure cooker; stir.

6   Pour the mixture over the chicken, top with the cilantro, and serve.

Mary's Chicken and Spaghetti

A dish handed down for generations from my familly friends—and it's so easy. Juicy and tender chicken in a simple garlic-tomato sauce. Layer Parmesan cheese then drizzle with butter.

Serves 4

4 bone-in chicken thighs, trimmed of fat

1 teaspoon kosher salt

¼ teaspoon freshly ground black pepper

1 tablespoon garlic powder

1 tablespoon extra-virgin olive oil

2 ounces unsalted butter, plus additional melted unsalted butter for drizzling

1 (28-ounce) can tomato sauce

1 pound angel hair pasta

1 cup shredded Parmesan cheese

1 Rinse and trim the chicken thighs, and sprinkle with the kosher salt, pepper, and garlic powder.

2 Heat the olive oil and unsalted butter in the pressure cooker with the lid off, add the chicken, and brown on both sides.

3 Add the tomato sauce; secure the lid.

4 When pressure is achieved, set a timer for 30 minutes.

5 When the cook time is complete and pressure is fully released, remove the lid with caution.

6 Cook the angel hair and drain in a colander.

7 Place the pasta on a platter, sprinkle with the cheese, and drizzle melted unsalted butter on top; toss lightly.

8 Serve the chicken and sauce over the pasta.

Chicken Piccata

This northern Italian favorite is delicious served over linguini. Italian Green Beans (page 198) round out a great meal.

Serves 4

1 tablespoon extra-virgin olive oil

4 boneless, skinless chicken breasts

½ teaspoon garlic kosher salt

½ teaspoon freshly ground black pepper

1 shallot, minced

Fresh juice and zest from 1 lemon

½ cup white wine

½ cup chicken stock

1 teaspoon cornstarch, dissolved in 1 tablespoon chicken stock

1 tablespoon sliced green olives

1 tablespoon capers

1 tablespoon chopped fresh parsley

1   Preheat the pressure cooker, add the oil, and heat for an additional 2 minutes. Season the chicken with the garlic kosher salt and pepper.

2   Add the chicken breasts to the pressure cooker a couple at a time to brown well. Pour off the excess fat.

3   Add the shallot, lemon juice and zest, wine, and stock to the pressure cooker; secure the lid.

4   When pressure is achieved, set a timer for 10 minutes.

5   When the cook time is complete and pressure is fully released, remove the lid with caution.

6   Transfer the chicken to platter and, with the lid off, stir in the dissolved cornstarch until the sauce thickens.

7   Add the olives, capers, and parsley. Pour the sauce over the chicken and serve hot.

Moroccan Chicken

The spices in this recipe alone would draw me to this fascinating country. Serve with Israeli couscous for a total Middle Eastern experience.

Serves 4 to 6

3 pounds skinless, bone-in chicken pieces

2 tablespoons extra-virgin olive oil

1 teaspoon kosher salt

1 teaspoon cumin seeds

1 cup chicken stock

1 medium onion, sliced

3 saffron strands

1 teaspoon turmeric powder

1 tablespoon lemon zest

¼ cup fresh lemon juice

12 black olives, pitted

4 quarters of preserved lemons (optional)

2 tablespoons chopped fresh cilantro

1　Pat the chicken dry using paper towels.

2　Preheat the oil in a pressure cooker with the lid off.

3　Place the chicken pieces into the pressure cooker and season with the kosher salt and cumin.

4　Cook the chicken for 3 minutes on each side, or until browned.

5　Transfer the chicken to a platter and add the stock to the pan; scrape up all the little bits from the bottom.

6　Place the chicken back into the pressure cooker with the onion, saffron, turmeric, lemon zest, lemon juice, olives and preserved lemons; secure the lid.

7　When pressure is achieved, set a timer for 20 minutes.

8　When the cook time is complete and pressure is fully released, remove the lid with caution.

9　Top the chicken with the cilantro and serve.

20 min.

Kickin' BBQ Chicken

Undeniably delicious next to a side of macaroni and cheese! The kids will actually come to the table for this meal. Just get out plenty of napkins.

Serves 4 to 6

1 whole chicken, cut into 8 pieces

½ cup chicken stock

1 teaspoon kosher salt

1 teaspoon freshly ground black pepper

1 teaspoon dry mustard

1 teaspoon paprika

½ teaspoon cayenne pepper

1 medium onion, diced

3 garlic cloves, minced

2 tablespoons cider vinegar

¼ cup brown sugar

¼ cup ketchup

¼ cup molasses

1   Place all ingredients into the pressure cooker; secure the lid.

2   When pressure is achieved, set a timer for 20 minutes.

3   When the cook time is complete and pressure is fully released, open the lid with caution.

4   Transfer the chicken to a broiler pan, bone side down.

5   Preheat the broiler on high.

6   To reduce the cooking liquid in the pressure cooker, with the lid off, turn on the pressure cooker and set the timer for 10 minutes; let cook with the lid off until the liquid turns into a syrup-like glaze.

7   While the liquid is reducing, place the chicken under the broiler for 7 minutes on each side.

8   Pour the sauce over the chicken and serve with additional sauce on the side.

Quinoa Turkey Meatloaf

Try this take on a yummy gluten-free meatloaf.
The kids will never guess it's good for them, and it
makes a great sandwich if there are leftovers.

Serves 4 to 6

⅓ cup cooked quinoa

⅔ cup chicken stock

1 medium onion, chopped

4 ounces mushrooms, sliced

1 tablespoon Worcestershire sauce

1 pound ground turkey

1 teaspoon kosher salt

½ teaspoon freshly ground black pepper

1 large egg, beaten

1 cup water

1 cup tomato sauce

¼ cup brown sugar

1   In a 2-quart stainless steel bowl, combine the quinoa, stock, onion, mushrooms, Worcestershire sauce, ground turkey, kosher salt, pepper, and egg; mix well using your hands.

2   Add the water to the pressure cooker.

3   Add the meatloaf mixture to the pressure cooker.

4   Combine the tomato sauce and brown sugar, then pour it over the meatloaf; secure the pressure cooker lid.

5   When pressure is achieved, set a timer for 20 minutes.

6   When the cook time is complete and pressure is fully released, remove the lid with caution.

7   Serve immediately.

Chipotle Chicken Burritos

South of the border flavors for a weeknight, wrapped nicely in a tortilla! Let the kids make their own burritos for added fun.

Serves 4 to 6

4 boneless, skinless chicken breasts, chopped into 1-inch pieces

1 cup chicken stock

2 whole chipotles in adobo sauce

1 teaspoon cumin seeds

1 teaspoon kosher salt

1 teaspoon freshly ground black pepper

1 teaspoon sugar

1 (10-ounce) can Mexican tomatoes with green chilis and lime

1 cup jasmine rice

1 cup canned black beans, drained

Six 12-inch flour tortillas

½ cup shredded Cheddar cheese

2 tablespoons chopped fresh cilantro

Lettuce, avocado, and sour cream for serving

1   Place the chicken, stock, chipotles, cumin, kosher salt, pepper, sugar, tomatoes, rice, and beans into the pressure cooker; secure the lid.

2   When pressure is achieved, set a timer for 10 minutes.

3   When the cook time is complete and pressure is fully released, remove the lid with caution.

4   To assemble the burritos, spoon the chicken mixture down the center of each tortilla, sprinkle with the cheese and cilantro, and roll them up.

5   Serve the burritos with the lettuce, avocado, and sour cream.

Stuffed Turkey Breast

This is a great Thanksgiving-style meal for two. Relax instead of spending all day in the kitchen, and save the leftovers for sandwiches!

Serves 4 to 6

2 pounds turkey breast tenderloins, unsalted butterflied

½ teaspoon kosher salt

¼ teaspoon poultry seasoning

½ cup dried cherries

One 6-ounce box turkey stuffing mix, prepared according to the package directions

1 cup chicken stock

1 envelope turkey gravy mix

1 Sprinkle the turkey with the kosher salt and poultry seasoning.

2 Add the dried cherries to the prepared stuffing.

3 Divide the stuffing between the tenderloins and place the mixture in the center of each tenderloin.

4 Roll the tenderloins to enclose the stuffing and secure with toothpicks.

5 Add the stock and gravy mix to a pressure cooker.

6 Place the tenderloins, toothpick side down, into the pressure cooker; secure the lid.

7 When pressure is achieved, set a timer for 20 minutes.

8 When the cook time is complete and pressure is fully released, remove the lid with caution.

9 Transfer the turkey to a cutting board.

10 Remove the toothpicks, cut each tenderloin into 1-inch rounds, and serve with the gravy.

12 min.

Stuffed Peppers with Couscous

These stuffed peppers are a lighter version of the original with rice. Perfect to take as leftovers for lunch; your coworkers will be jealous.

Serves 4

1 pound ground turkey

1 teaspoon kosher salt

1 teaspoon freshly ground black pepper

1 medium sweet onion, chopped

3 garlic cloves, minced

4 saffron threads

One 14.5-ounce can petite diced tomatoes

½ cup Israeli couscous

1 cup chicken stock

4 large bell peppers, seeds and membrane removed

1 cup tomato sauce

¼ cup grated Parmesan cheese

1   Place the turkey into the pressure cooker and cook with the lid off for 3 minutes, breaking the meat up using a wooden spoon.

2   Season the turkey with the kosher salt and pepper, add the onion to the pressure cooker, and cook for an additional 3 minutes.

3   Add the garlic and saffron to the pressure cooker and cook for an additional minute.

4   Add the tomatoes, couscous, and stock to the pressure cooker; stir, then secure the lid.

5   When pressure is achieved, set a timer for 6 minutes.

6   When the cook time is complete and pressure is fully released, remove the lid with caution.

7   Divide the turkey mixture among the peppers.

8   Rinse the pressure cooker insert, place the peppers into the pressure cooker, and cover them with tomato sauce and Parmesan cheese; secure the lid.

9   When pressure is achieved, set a timer for 6 minutes.

10 When the cook time is complete and pressure is fully released, remove the lid with caution.

11 Serve immediately.

Turkey Pot Roast

A great one-pot dish that anyone can make. You will definitely add this to your favorites. This Turkey Pot Roast makes for amazing leftovers or the beginnings of turkey pot pie.

Serves 4 to 6

1 boneless turkey breast (about 4 pounds), rinsed

½ teaspoon sea kosher salt

½ teaspoon freshly ground black pepper

½ teaspoon poultry seasoning

1 tablespoon extra-virgin olive oil

1 medium onion, quartered

¼ cup sliced mushrooms

½ cup amber beer

½ cup chicken stock

1 tablespoon tomato paste

2 celery stalks, diced

2 sprigs fresh thyme

3 carrots, peeled, cut into 2-inch pieces

4 red bliss potatoes, halved

1 Pat the turkey breast dry using paper towels.

2 Rub the turkey breast with kosher salt, pepper, and poultry seasoning.

3 Preheat the olive oil in a pressure cooker with the lid off.

4 Gently place the turkey breast into the pressure cooker; sear for about 10 minutes until all sides are golden brown.

5 Transfer the turkey breast to a platter.

6 Add the onions and mushrooms to the pressure cooker; cook for 2 minutes.

7 Add the beer and stock to deglaze the bottom of the pressure cooker; scrape up all the little bits.

8 Return the turkey to the pressure cooker, along with the tomato paste, celery, and thyme; stir, then secure the lid.

9 When pressure is achieved, set a timer for 45 minutes.

10 When the cook time is complete and pressure is fully released, remove the lid with caution.

11 Add the carrots and potatoes to the pressure cooker; secure lid.

12 When pressure is achieved, set a timer for 10 minutes.

13 When the cook time is complete and pressure is fully released, remove the lid with caution.

14 Remove and discard the thyme and serve.

Thai Chicken Curry

This is a fun recipe to expand your palate in a simple, easy way. The exotic flavors will delight you. It's delicious served with jasmine rice.

Serves 4 to 6

2 cups chicken stock

1 medium onion, diced

3 garlic cloves, sliced

1 tablespoon fresh ginger, peeled and sliced

2 tablespoons Thai red curry paste

1 tablespoon lime zest

2 tablespoons fish sauce

2 pounds boneless chicken tenders

2 tablespoons brown sugar

1 red bell pepper, julienned

One 13.5-ounce can light coconut milk

One 8-ounce can bamboo shoots, drained

2 tablespoons chopped fresh cilantro for garnish

Chopped green onions for garnish

Cooked jasmine rice for serving

1   Place the stock, onion, garlic, ginger, curry paste, lime zest, fish sauce, chicken, brown sugar, bell pepper, coconut milk, and bamboo shoots into the pressure cooker; secure the lid.

2   When pressure is achieved, set a timer for 10 minutes.

3   When the cook time is complete and pressure is fully released, remove the lid with caution.

4   Top with the cilantro and green onions, and serve over jasmine rice.

Beef and Lamb

Salisbury Steak

Ground beef combined with some pantry ingredients
results in a simple and delicious meal in minutes.
So easy and so good!

Serves 6 to 8

2 pounds lean ground beef

1 small onion, minced

1 teaspoon steak seasoning

1 teaspoon kosher salt

½ teaspoon freshly ground
black pepper

1 teaspoon Worcestershire sauce

1 tablespoon extra-virgin olive oil

1 large sweet onion, thinly sliced

8 ounces mushrooms, sliced

½ cup beef stock

1 (10.5-ounce) can cream of
mushroom soup

Cooked noodles for serving

1   In a large bowl, mix the beef, onion, steak seasoning,
kosher salt, pepper, and Worcestershire sauce.

2   Form the mixture into equal-size patties.

3   Preheat the pressure cooker, add the oil, and then
brown patties for 3 minutes per side.

4   Add the onion, mushrooms, stock, and cream of
mushroom soup to the pressure cooker; secure the lid.

5   When pressure is achieved, set a timer for 20 minutes.

6   When the cook time is complete and pressure is fully
released, remove the lid with caution.

7   Serve over noodles.

Ropa Vieja

This Cuban dish is delicious next to yellow rice and beans and garnished with salsa and sour cream. The leftovers are the perfect start to make incredible burritos.

Serves 4 to 6

2 pounds flank steak

1 medium onion, peeled and halved

4 garlic cloves, minced

1 cup beef stock

1 teaspoon cumin

½ teaspoon ground coriander

1 envelope Sazon seasoning

½ cup red wine

One 14.5-ounce can petite diced tomatoes

1 green bell pepper, diced

2 tablespoon chopped fresh cilantro

¼ cup capers

1   Place the steak, onion, garlic, stock, cumin, coriander, Sazon seasoning, and wine into the pressure cooker; secure the lid.

2   When pressure is achieved, set a timer for 40 minutes.

3   When the cook time is complete and pressure is fully released, remove the lid with caution.

4   Shred the beef using two forks and add the tomatoes, bell pepper, cilantro, and capers to the pressure cooker; secure the lid.

5   When pressure is achieved, set a timer for 20 minutes.

6   When the cook time is complete and pressure is fully release, remove the lid with caution.

7   Serve immediately.

Beef Enchiladas

The enchilada kit features tortillas and sauce, which you can buy individually if you prefer. If doing so, make sure you use a teaspoon each of cumin and coriander when cooking the meat!

Serves 4

1 flank steak

1 cup beef stock

1 enchilada kit

1 cup shredded Cheddar cheese, divided

Sour cream and chopped green onions for garnish

1 Place the steak, stock, and seasoning mix from the enchilada kit into the pressure cooker; secure the lid.

2 When pressure is achieved, set a timer for 60 minutes.

3 When the cook time is complete and pressure is fully released, remove the lid with caution.

4 Shred the beef with two forks.

5 Lay the tortillas from the dinner kit on a cutting board and sprinkle with half of the cheese.

6 Add the shredded steak to each tortilla and roll up.

7 Pour the enchilada sauce from the dinner kit over each enchilada and top with the remaining cheese.

8 Microwave the enchiladas for 1 minute, or until the cheese is melted.

9 Top with the sour cream and green onions, and serve immediately.

Beef Stroganoff

This delicious dish, stocked with bits of beef, mushroom, and cream, can be paired with a cold beer and dinner salad for a Russian-style meal. To spare some calories, feel free to use leaner cuts of meat. When tenderized to perfection in the pressure cooker, you'd never taste the difference.

Serves 2

1 tablespoon all-purpose flour

1 teaspoon kosher salt

½ teaspoon freshly ground black pepper

1 pound beef sirloin, cut into 1-inch pieces

1 medium onion, chopped

2 garlic cloves, minced

1 pound mushrooms, sliced

1 sprig fresh thyme

1 cup beef stock

1 teaspoon Worcestershire sauce

1 cup sour cream

2 cups cooked and buttered noodles for serving

1. In a bowl, combine the flour, kosher salt, and pepper.

2. Roll the beef pieces in the flour mixture; shake off excess.

3. Add the beef, onion, garlic, mushrooms, thyme, stock, and Worcestershire sauce to the pressure cooker; secure the lid.

4. When pressure is achieved, set a timer for 20 minutes.

5. When the cook time is complete and pressure is fully released, remove the lid with caution.

6. Remove and discard the thyme and stir in the sour cream.

7. Serve over the buttered noodles.

Carolina BBQ Brisket

Switch up your barbecue sauces to intensify the flavors in this tender brisket. You can serve this Southern favorite with creamy grits and pickled jalapeños for a guaranteed crowd pleaser.

Serves 6

3 pounds beef brisket, trimmed

1 cup beef stock

1 cup apple cider

1 teaspoon cider vinegar

1 teaspoon kosher salt

½ teaspoon freshly ground black pepper

2 cups barbecue sauce

1 Place the brisket, stock, cider, vinegar, kosher salt, and pepper into the pressure cooker; secure the lid.

2 When pressure is achieved, set a timer for 60 minutes.

3 When the cook time is complete and pressure is fully released, remove the lid with caution.

4 Remove the brisket to a platter.

5 With the lid off, simmer the cooking liquid for about 10 minutes, until it is reduced by half.

6 Cut the brisket into 2-inch pieces and place the meat back into the pressure cooker.

7 Add the barbecue sauce to the pressure cooker, heat until warm, and serve.

Braised Lamb Shanks

A delicious dish of juicy, tender lamb cooked in a savory sauce. Serve it with creamy polenta and a crisp garden salad.

Serves 2 to 4

4 meaty lamb shanks, cut into 3-inch pieces

1 teaspoon kosher salt

½ teaspoon freshly ground black pepper

1 sprig fresh thyme

1 teaspoon fresh rosemary, chopped

3 tablespoons extra-virgin olive oil

1 medium onion, chopped

3 medium carrots, peeled and chopped

2 garlic cloves, minced

½ cup dry red wine

1 cup drained canned diced tomatoes

2 cups beef stock

1 Rub the lamb with the kosher salt, pepper, thyme, and rosemary.

2 Place the lamb into pressure cooker, along with the olive oil, onion, carrots, garlic, wine, tomatoes, and stock; secure the lid.

3 When pressure is achieved, set a timer for 45 minutes.

4 When the cook time is complete and pressure is fully released, remove the lid with caution.

5 Serve immediately.

50 min.

French Dip Sandwich

This is an all-star game-day recipe for a classic sandwich. I'm not sure which is better: the tender, flavorful meat or the juice for dipping. Be sure to toast the rolls for added texture.

Serves 4

1 bottom round roast
(about 2 pounds),
cut into 1-inch slices

1 cup beef stock

1 tablespoon Worcestershire
sauce

1 garlic clove, sliced

1 large sweet onion, quartered

1 tablespoon grape jelly

½ teaspoon kosher salt

½ teaspoon freshly ground
black pepper

1 sprig fresh thyme

4 French rolls, sliced in half
and toasted

1 Place the roast, stock, Worcestershire sauce, garlic, onion, jelly, kosher salt, pepper, and thyme into the pressure cooker; secure the lid.

2 When pressure is achieved, set a timer for 50 minutes.

3 When the cook time is complete and pressure is fully released, remove the lid with caution.

4 Remove and discard the thyme.

5 Divide the meat slices among the French rolls.

6 Serve with a dish of the meat juice from the pressure cooker as a dipping sauce.

Corned Beef and Cabbage

The luck of the Irish can be served up without the hassle. Use a dry stout, like Guinness, for the beer in this recipe. Then pour yourself a pint to savor the notes in this traditional dish.

Serves 4 to 6

3 pounds corned beef, trimmed

1 large onion, quartered

½ cup beef stock

1 bottle (12 ounces) dark beer

½ teaspoon mustard seeds

½ teaspoon whole black peppercorns

2 allspice berries

1 bay leaf

1 teaspoon dry mustard

3 garlic cloves, minced

6 small onions, peeled

6 small red bliss potatoes, halved

12 baby carrots

1 head cabbage, cut into 6 wedges

1. Place the corned beef, large onion, stock, beer, mustard seeds, peppercorns, allspice, bay leaf, mustard powder and garlic into the pressure cooker; secure the lid.

2. When pressure is achieved, set a timer for 70 minutes.

3. When the cook time is complete and pressure is fully released, remove the lid with caution.

4. Remove and discard the bay leaf and add the onions, potatoes, carrots, and cabbage to the pressure cooker; secure the lid.

5. When pressure is achieved, set a timer for 7 minutes.

6. When the cook time is complete and pressure is fully released, remove the lid with caution.

7. Serve immediately.

45 min.

Corned Beef Reuben

Bring this delicatessen special to your kitchen table without leaving the house. In a pinch, you can make your own Thousand Island dressing with 2 parts mayo, 1 part ketchup, and 2 parts sweet pickle relish.

Serves 4

1 corned beef brisket (about 2 pounds), sliced ½-inch thick

1 medium onion, quartered

1 carrot, peeled and chopped into 2-inch pieces

½ cup water

1 teaspoon mustard seeds

1 bay leaf

1 cup drained sauerkraut

8 slices rye bread, toasted

4 slices Swiss cheese

2 tablespoons Thousand Island dressing

1   Place the corned beef, onion, carrot, water, mustard seeds, and bay leaf into the pressure cooker; secure the lid.

2   When pressure is achieved, set a timer for 45 minutes.

3   Meanwhile, divide the sauerkraut among 4 bread slices, then top each slice with 1 slice of cheese and ½ tablespoon of Thousand Island dressing.

4   When the cook time is complete and pressure is fully released, remove the lid with caution.

5   Remove and discard the bay leaf.

6   Divide the corned beef among the prepared slices of bread and top each with another slice of bread.

7   Serve immediately.

Spicy Italian Meatloaf

I'm tired of meatloaf getting a bad rap. Try this tender and delicious twist on a classic dish. It's oh-so-good with Garlic Mashed Potatoes (page 183) and fresh garden peas. It's even more delicious packed into a leftover hoagie.

Serves 4 to 6

1 medium onion, thinly sliced

3 garlic cloves, minced

¼ cup fresh bread crumbs

¼ cup heavy cream

2 large eggs, beaten

1½ pounds ground chuck

½ pound ground pork

¼ cup grated Parmesan cheese

1 tablespoon Italian seasoning

1 teaspoon kosher salt

1 teaspoon freshly ground black pepper

½ teaspoon crushed red pepper flakes

2 cups beef stock

2 cups pasta sauce, divided

1 cup shredded mozzarella cheese

1 In a large bowl, combine the onion, garlic, bread crumbs, cream, and eggs; mix well and let rest for 5 minutes.

2 Add the chuck, pork, Parmesan cheese, Italian seasoning, kosher salt, pepper, and red pepper flakes to the bowl; mix well and shape into a loaf.

3 Pour the stock into the pressure cooker.

4 Fit the pressure cooker with a stainless steel rack and place the loaf on the rack; cover the loaf with 1 cup of pasta sauce and secure the lid.

5 When pressure is achieved, set a timer for 20 minutes.

6 When the cook time is complete and pressure is fully released, remove the lid with caution.

7 Pour the remaining 1 cup pasta sauce over the loaf and sprinkle with the mozzarella cheese; secure lid.

8 When pressure is achieved, set a timer for 10 minutes.

9 When the cook time is complete and pressure is fully released, remove the lid with caution.

10 Serve immediately.

Holiday Brisket with Root Vegetables

Not just for Hanukkah! This is the most tender brisket you will ever taste, packed with veggies and flavor. This Holiday Brisket is a true comfort food for a cold winter night.

Serves 4 to 6

2 tablespoons extra-virgin olive oil

1 first-cut brisket (about 3 pounds), trimmed

1 teaspoon kosher salt

1 teaspoon freshly ground black pepper

½ cup port wine

1 cup beef stock

1 cup sliced sweet onion

1 sprig fresh thyme

4 allspice berries

1 bay leaf

1 tablespoon tomato paste

½ cup peeled and diced celery root

½ cup peeled and sliced carrot

½ cup peeled and sliced parsnip

1. Preheat the oil in a pressure cooker over medium-high heat.

2. Season the brisket with kosher salt and pepper.

3. Add the brisket to the sauté pan and brown 3 minutes on each side.

4. Transfer the brisket to a platter and drain the grease from the pan.

5. Add the wine and stock to deglaze the pan; scrape up all the little bits from the bottom.

6. Return the brisket to the pressure cooker. Add the onions, thyme, allspice berries, bay leaf, and tomato paste to the pressure cooker; secure the lid.

7. When pressure is achieved, set a timer for 60 minutes.

8. When the cook time is complete and pressure is fully released, remove the lid with caution.

9. Remove and discard the thyme and bay leaf.

10. Add the celery root, carrot, and parsnip to the pressure cooker; secure the lid.

11. When pressure is achieved, set a timer for 5 minutes.

12. When the cook time is complete and pressure is fully released, remove the lid with caution.

13. Cut the brisket against the grain and serve.

Beef Short Ribs

Beef Short Ribs are one of life's greatest pleasures for the meat and potato lover. Juicy and tender, melt-in-your-mouth goodness. Serve with warm polenta for a hearty meal.

Serves 6 to 8

1 tablespoon extra-virgin olive oil

4 to 6 pounds beef short ribs, cut into individual ribs

½ teaspoon kosher salt

1 cup beef stock

1 cup dry red wine

2 teaspoons chopped fresh rosemary

3 medium onions, chopped

4 garlic cloves, minced

1 (28-ounce) can whole tomatoes with juice

2 tablespoons Worcestershire sauce

2 cups frozen pearl onions

1 pound baby carrots

1   Preheat the pressure cooker, add the olive oil, and heat for 2 minutes. Season the ribs with kosher salt and place into the pressure cooker.

2   Brown the ribs on each side, about 5 minutes per side.

3   Add the stock, wine, and rosemary to the pressure cooker; secure the lid.

4   When pressure is achieved, set a timer for 45 minutes.

5   When the cook time is complete and pressure is fully released, remove the lid with caution.

6   Using a skimmer, remove as much of the fat from the stock as possible.

7   Add the onions, garlic, tomatoes, Worcestershire sauce, pearl onions, and carrots to the pressure cooker; secure the lid.

8   When pressure is achieved, set a timer for 15 minutes.

9   When the cook time is complete and pressure is fully released, remove the lid with caution.

10   Serve immediately.

35 min.

Beef Goulash

To add further dimension to this classic dish, toast the caraway seeds first. Serve over spaetzli or noodles.

Serves 4 to 6

2 pounds beef stew meat

1 medium onion, sliced

2 garlic cloves, minced

1½ cups beef stock

½ cup tomato paste

2 tablespoons Worcestershire sauce

1 tablespoon brown sugar

2 teaspoons kosher salt

2 teaspoons Hungarian sweet paprika

1 tablespoon caraway seeds

1 Place all of the ingredients into the pressure cooker; secure the lid.

2 When pressure is achieved, set a timer for 35 minutes.

3 When the cook time is complete and pressure is fully released, remove the lid with caution.

4 Serve immediately.

Stuffed Cabbage

An old-fashioned favorite you'll have time to make even during the week. Great for leftovers if there are any!

Serves 6

1 large head cabbage

1 pound extra-lean ground beef or ground turkey

½ cup minced onion

2 garlic cloves, minced

1 teaspoon kosher salt

1 teaspoon freshly ground black pepper

1 large egg, beaten

1 tablespoon Worcestershire sauce

1 cup cooked rice

1 (8-ounce) can tomato sauce

1 tablespoon sugar

1 teaspoon beef stock

2 cups shredded mozzarella cheese

1 Separate the cabbage into 12 large leaves.

2 Boil or steam the cabbage until flexible, but not mushy. Drain and cool.

3 In a medium bowl, combine the beef, onion, garlic, kosher salt, pepper, egg, and Worcestershire sauce.

4 Add the rice to the bowl and mix well.

5 Place ¼ cup of the beef mixture in the center of each cabbage leaf.

6 Fold in the sides of each leaf and roll the ends over the meat. Transfer to the pressure cooker.

7 In a small bowl, combine the tomato sauce, sugar, and stock.

8 Pour the sauce mixture over the cabbage rolls in the pressure cooker; secure the lid.

9 When pressure is achieved, set a timer for 15 minutes.

10 When the cook time is complete and pressure is fully released, remove the lid with caution.

11 Sprinkle with the cheese. When the cheese is melted, serve.

Moroccan Lamb Shanks

Embark on an exotic adventure without leaving your own kitchen! The aroma of the spices will bring everyone to the table.

Serves 4

2 tablespoons extra-virgin olive oil

4 lamb shanks

½ teaspoon kosher salt

½ teaspoon freshly ground black pepper

½ cup dry red wine

½ cup chicken stock

2 tablespoons tomato paste

½ cup diced carrots

1 shallot, minced

3 garlic cloves, minced

½ teaspoon cumin seeds

½ teaspoon pumpkin pie spice

One 16.5-ounce can petite diced tomatoes

2 tablespoons chopped fresh cilantro

1   Preheat the olive oil in a pressure cooker with the lid off.

2   Season the lamb shanks with the kosher salt and pepper.

3   Add the lamb to the pressure cooker and sear each shank on all sides until browned.

4   Drain the fat from the pan and add the wine to deglaze the pan, scraping up all the little bits from the bottom.

5   Add the stock, tomato paste, carrots, shallot, garlic, cumin, pumpkin pie spice, and tomatoes to the pressure cooker; secure the lid.

6   When pressure is achieved, set a timer for 60 minutes.

7   When the cook time is complete and pressure is fully released, remove the lid with caution.

8   Top with the cilantro and serve.

Italian Pot Roast

Add a new twist to your Sunday dinner. Serve Italian Pot Roast over your favorite pasta, and feel free to break out the Chianti to wash it down.

60 min.

Serves 4 to 6

2 tablespoons extra-virgin olive oil

1 chuck roast (about 4 pounds)

1 teaspoon kosher salt

½ teaspoon freshly ground black pepper

¼ cup dry red wine

1 cup beef stock

1 medium onion, sliced

3 garlic cloves, sliced

1 bell pepper, julienned

½ cup giardiniera pickled vegetables

1 teaspoon garlic powder

1 teaspoon Italian seasoning

1 bay leaf

One 28-ounce jar pasta sauce

Cooked pasta or polenta for serving

1. Preheat the olive oil in a pressure cooker with the lid off.

2. Season the roast with kosher salt and pepper.

3. Add the roast to the pressure cooker and sear for 3 minutes on each side.

4. Remove the roast to a platter and drain the fat from the pan.

5. Add the wine and stock to deglaze the bottom of the pressure cooker; scrape up all the little bits from the bottom.

6. Return the roast to the pressure cooker, along with the onions, garlic, bell pepper, giardiniera, garlic powder, Italian seasoning, and bay leaf; secure the lid.

7. When pressure is achieved, set a timer for 60 minutes.

8. When the cook time is complete and pressure is fully released, remove the lid with caution.

9. Remove and discard the bay leaf, then add the pasta sauce to the pressure cooker; secure the lid.

10. When pressure is achieved, set a timer for 6 minutes.

11. When the cook time is complete and pressure is fully released, remove the lid with caution.

12. Serve immediately over pasta or polenta.

Meatballs for Spaghetti

You will never experience a meatball lighter or more tender—these are more like a dumpling than the classic version. This recipe will impress even your Italian friends.

Serves 6 to 8

MEATBALLS

1½ cups fresh bread crumbs

4 cups beef stock, divided

1 pound ground chuck

1½ pounds ground pork

3 garlic cloves, minced

1 small onion, minced

¾ cup grated Romano cheese

1 teaspoon kosher salt

½ teaspoon freshly ground black pepper

2 large eggs, beaten

SAUCE

4 tablespoons tomato paste

2 (28-ounce) cans Italian tomatoes

3 garlic cloves, minced

1 small onion, minced

1 teaspoon dried oregano

1 teaspoon dried basil

1 tablespoon unsalted butter

Cooked spaghetti for serving

FOR THE MEATBALLS:

1. In a bowl, soak the breadcrumbs in 2 cups of stock.

2. Pour the remaining 2 cups of stock into a pressure cooker.

3. Add the chuck, pork, garlic, onion, cheese, kosher salt, pepper, and eggs to the breadcrumb mixture; mix and form into 2-inch meatballs.

4. Place the meatballs into the pressure cooker; secure the lid.

5. When pressure is achieved, set a timer for 20 minutes.

6. When the cook time is complete and pressure is fully released, remove the lid with caution.

7. Transfer the meatballs to a platter, and pour the stock into a separate bowl; skim off the fat.

FOR THE SAUCE:

1. For the sauce: Dissolve the tomato paste in the skimmed stock and pour it into the pressure cooker.

2. Add the tomatoes, garlic, onion, oregano, basil, and unsalted butter to the pressure cooker.

3. To finish, add the meatballs to the sauce mixture in the pressure cooker; secure the lid.

4. When pressure is achieved, set a timer for 15 minutes.

5. When the cook time is complete and pressure is fully released, remove the lid with caution.

6. Serve over spaghetti.

Osso Buco

This is a classic recipe in the simplest way. No one will believe you cooked this scrumptious dish in under an hour. They will think you spent the whole day in the kitchen! Because of the pressure cooker's ability to deliver tender, juicy meat, feel free to substitute beef or lamb shanks instead of veal.

Serves 4

2 pounds meaty veal shanks

½ cup diced onion

½ cup diced celery

½ cup peeled and diced parsnip

2 garlic cloves, minced

1 teaspoon kosher salt

½ teaspoon freshly ground black pepper

½ cup vermouth

One 14.5-ounce can petite diced tomatoes

1 sprig fresh thyme

1 teaspoon orange zest

1 cup beef stock

1   Place all of the ingredients into the pressure cooker; secure the lid.

2   When pressure is achieved, set a timer for 40 minutes.

3   When the cook time is complete and pressure is fully released, remove the lid with caution.

4   Remove the thyme and transfer the veal to a platter.

5   With the lid off, reduce the sauce for 10 minutes.

6   Using an immersion blender, pulse until the sauce reaches a desired consistency, then pour it over the veal shanks and serve.

Porcupine Balls

Rice meatballs just like when you were a kid!
This throwback brings back the good ol' days.
Your kids will love them.

Serves 4 to 6

1 pound ground chuck

½ cup dry white rice

½ cup water

1 small onion, minced

1 teaspoon kosher salt

½ teaspoon celery kosher salt

¼ teaspoon garlic powder

½ teaspoon freshly ground
black pepper

1½ cups beef stock

2 cups tomato sauce

2 teaspoons Worcestershire sauce

1   In a bowl, combine the chuck, rice, water, onion, kosher salt, celery kosher salt, garlic powder, and pepper.

2   Shape the mixture into 2-inch balls.

3   Add the meatballs and stock to the pressure cooker; secure the lid.

4   When pressure is achieved, set a timer for 15 minutes.

5   When the cook time is complete and pressure is fully released, remove the lid with caution.

6   Transfer the porcupine balls to a platter.

7   Add the tomato sauce and Worcestershire sauce to the pressure cooker.

8   With the lid open, heat sauce through.

9   Return the porcupine balls to the pressure cooker, stir, and serve.

Beef Kung Pao

Grab your chopsticks, because we're making that item you always order for Chinese take-out. You'll never order in again after making Beef Kung Pao for yourself.

Serves 4

1½ pounds round steak, sliced into strips

½ teaspoon kosher salt

¼ teaspoon white pepper

1 tablespoon sesame oil

2 garlic cloves, minced

¼ cup cashews

½ teaspoon crushed red pepper flakes

1 teaspoon minced ginger

1 large onion, sliced

½ cup beef stock

2 tablespoons cornstarch

¼ cup soy sauce

¼ cup orange juice

1 large red bell pepper, julienned

1 cup broccoli florets

Cooked basmati rice for serving

1 Pound the steak and cut it into ¼-inch strips; sprinkle with the kosher salt and white pepper.

2 Heat the sesame oil in the pressure cooker with the lid off, add the meat strips, and brown.

3 Add the garlic, cashews, red pepper flakes, ginger, and onion and cook for an additional minute.

4 Pour the stock into the pressure cooker; secure the lid.

5 When pressure is achieved, set a timer for 10 minutes.

6 When the cook time is complete and pressure is fully released, remove the lid with caution.

7 Mix the cornstarch with the soy sauce and orange juice, and stir into the meat mixture. Add the bell pepper and broccoli and let simmer until thickened.

8 Serve over rice.

50 min.

Stuffed Flank Steak

This stuffed steak roll is beautiful when sliced and served over squash ribbons. A friend of mine gave me a great tip: to get thinner slices, chill the meat before you slice, and reheat to serve.

Serves 4

1 flank steak (1½ to 2 pounds), unsalted butterflied

1 green bell pepper, sliced

1 small onion, sliced

¼ cup shredded Parmesan cheese

1 tablespoon olive oil, plus more for rubbing the steak

1 teaspoon Italian seasoning

1 teaspoon kosher salt

Pinch of freshly ground black pepper

1 cup beef stock

One 14.5-ounce can Italian seasoned stewed tomatoes

Cooked pasta or rice for serving

1 Open the butterflied flank steak.

2 Top with the bell pepper, onion, and cheese.

3 Roll up the steak and tie with butcher's twine.

4 Rub the steak roll with olive oil, Italian seasoning, kosher salt, and pepper.

5 In a sauté pan, heat the olive oil, and brown the steak roll all over. Remove the steak roll to a plate.

6 Pour a small amount of stock into the pan to deglaze, then pour the contents of the pan into the pressure cooker. Add the remaining stock and tomatoes; secure the pressure cooker lid.

7 When pressure is achieved, set a timer for 50 minutes.

8 When the cook time is complete and pressure is fully released, remove the lid with caution.

9 Let the steak roll rest on a platter for 20 minutes.

10 Remove the twine and cut the roll into ½-inch slices.

11 Pour sauce over the flank steak and serve over pasta or rice.

Sunday Pot Roast

This pot roast is just like the one Grandma made on Sunday, cooking all day, but you can make it anytime. Now you'll have more time to spend with the family.

Serves 4 to 6

3 pounds chuck roast

1 teaspoon kosher salt

½ teaspoon freshly ground black pepper

2 cups beef stock

1 cup tomato juice

2 small onions, peeled and halved

1 sprig fresh thyme

1 sprig fresh rosemary

1 tablespoon Worcestershire sauce

8 new potatoes, halved

4 carrots, peeled and cut into 2-inch pieces

2 celery stalks, cut into 2-inch pieces

1   Place the chuck roast, kosher salt, pepper, stock, tomato juice, onions, thyme, rosemary, and Worcestershire sauce into the pressure cooker; secure the lid.

2   When pressure is achieved, set a timer for 60 minutes.

3   When the cook time is complete and pressure is fully released, remove the lid with caution.

4   Remove and discard the thyme and rosemary.

5   Add the potatoes, carrots, and celery to the pressure cooker; secure the lid.

6   When pressure is achieved, set a timer for 5 minutes.

7   When the cook time is complete and pressure is fully released, remove the lid with caution.

8   Serve immediately.

Swedish Meatballs

Everyone's favorite meatballs in a creamy sauce. Great as an appetizer or served over noodles. Swedish Meatballs are the perfect make-ahead dish to take to your next potluck party.

Serves 6 to 8

2 cups beef stock

1½ cups bread crumbs

½ cup heavy cream

1 pound ground chuck

½ pound ground pork

2 large eggs, beaten

1 small onion, minced

1 celery stalk, minced

2 teaspoons kosher salt

½ teaspoon freshly ground black pepper

¼ teaspoon ground allspice

1 cup sour cream

1   Preheat a pressure cooker, add the stock, and bring to a boil, about 5 minutes.

2   In a large bowl, soak the bread crumbs in heavy cream for 5 minutes.

3   Add the chuck, pork, eggs, onion, celery, kosher salt, pepper, and allspice to the bowl; mix well.

4   Shape the mixture into 1-inch meatballs.

5   Add the meatballs to the pressure cooker; secure the lid.

6   When pressure is achieved, set a timer for 10 minutes.

7   When the cook time is complete and pressure is fully released, remove the lid with caution.

8   Transfer the meatballs to a platter.

9   Add sour cream to the sauce in the pressure cooker, stir and pour over the meatballs.

10   Serve immediately.

Swiss Steak

An old-fashioned meal that families still enjoy. For those who like it, you can easily substitute venison or any other game meat.

Serves 4 to 6

1 tablespoon extra-virgin olive oil

2 pounds round steak, cut into 6 equal pieces

¼ teaspoon kosher salt

¼ teaspoon freshly ground black pepper

¼ teaspoon garlic powder

1 medium onion, thinly sliced

1 (28-ounce) can whole tomatoes, chopped

1 Preheat the olive oil in a pressure cooker with the lid off; season the meat with kosher salt, pepper, and garlic powder.

2 Add the meat to the pressure cooker and brown on both sides; add the onion and tomatoes; secure the lid.

3 When pressure is achieved, set a timer for 25 minutes.

4 When the cook time is complete and pressure is fully released, remove the lid with caution.

5 Serve immediately.

Braciole

Great for special occasions and dinner parties, this fancy, fast dish will be sure to impress your guests, but it's also easy enough to feed your family during the week. Serve over creamy polenta or your favorite pasta.

Serves 2 to 4

1 pound top sirloin, sliced very thin

½ cup unsalted butter, melted

1½ cups grated Parmesan cheese

1½ cups soft bread crumbs

1 teaspoon kosher salt

½ teaspoon freshly ground black pepper

1 tablespoon chopped fresh parsley

½ teaspoon garlic kosher salt

½ cup raisins

½ cup red wine

1 cup beef stock

1 sprig fresh thyme

⅛ teaspoon dried oregano

3 cups pasta sauce

1   Lay the steak slices on a cutting board.

2   In a bowl, combine the unsalted butter, cheese, bread crumbs, kosher salt, pepper, parsley, garlic kosher salt, and raisins; mix well.

3   Place 2 tablespoons of the raisin mixture on the bottom corner of each steak slice; roll up and secure with a toothpick.

4   Place the steak rolls, wine, stock, thyme, and oregano into the pressure cooker; secure the lid.

5   When pressure is achieved, set a timer for 20 minutes.

6   When the cook time is complete and pressure is fully released, remove the lid with caution.

7   Remove and discard the thyme, add the pasta sauce, and let the sauce heat through.

8   Serve immediately.

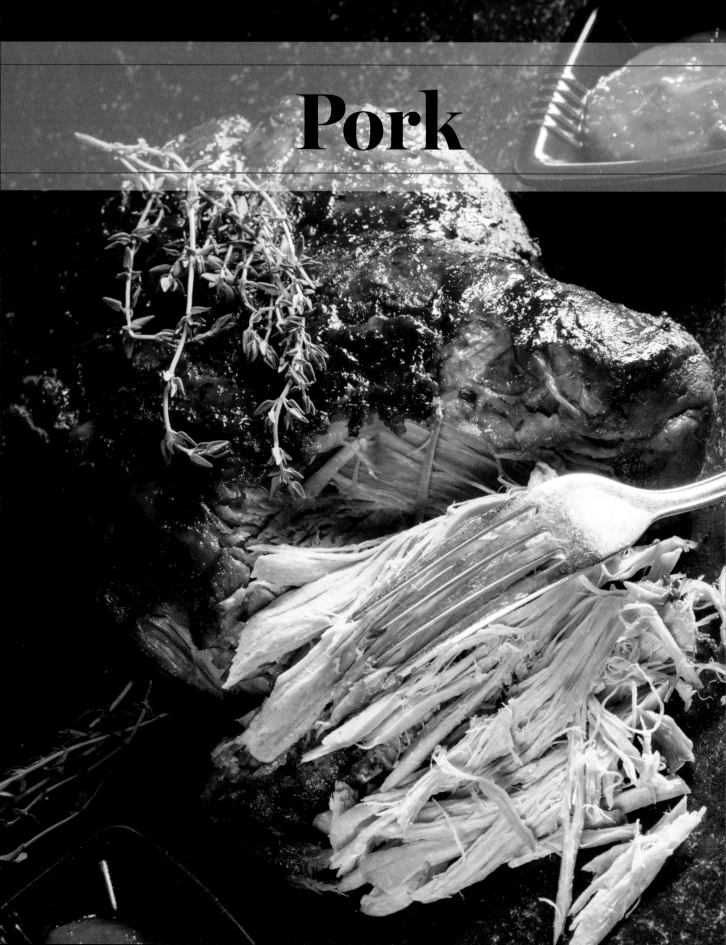

Pork

35 min.

Asian Pork Tenderloin

To satisfy your Far East cravings, pair this dish
with jasmine rice. The tenderloin is tender and juicy,
with a little bit of heat.

Serves 4 to 6

2 tablespoons extra-virgin olive oil

1 pork tenderloin (about 2 pounds)

1 teaspoon kosher salt

1 teaspoon freshly ground
black pepper

2 garlic cloves, minced

½ cup orange juice

½ cup chicken stock

½ cup sweet orange marmalade

2 tablespoons honey

1 tablespoon Asian hot garlic
sauce

1 Preheat the olive oil in the pressure cooker with
the lid off.

2 Season the pork with kosher salt and pepper and
add to the pressure cooker; brown on all sides.

3 Add the garlic and sauté for an additional minute.

4 Add the orange juice and stock to the pressure
cooker; secure the lid.

5 When pressure is achieved, set a timer for 15 minutes.

6 When the cook time is complete and pressure is fully
released, remove the lid with caution.

7 Add the orange marmalade, honey, and hot garlic
sauce to the pressure cooker; secure the lid.

8 When pressure is achieved, set a timer for 20 minutes.

9 When the cook time is complete and pressure is fully
released, remove the lid with caution.

10 Serve immediately.

Bangkok Baby Back Ribs

Better than takeout, I opt for these
Bangkok baby back ribs any day!
Luscious, sweet, and savory.

Serves 2 to 4

1 full slab baby back ribs

½ cup chicken stock

2 tablespoons sliced fresh ginger

1 medium onion, quartered

2 garlic cloves, minced

2 tablespoons sesame oil

2 tablespoons soy sauce

2 tablespoons rice wine vinegar

2 tablespoons brown sugar

1   Place the ribs, stock, ginger, onion, garlic, sesame oil, soy sauce, and vinegar into the pressure cooker; secure the lid.

2   When pressure is achieved, set a timer for 25 minutes.

3   When the cook time is complete and pressure is fully released, remove the lid with caution.

4   Transfer the ribs to a broiler pan, bone side down.

5   Preheat the broiler on high.

6   To reduce the cooking liquid, with the lid off, turn on the pressure cooker and set the timer for 10 minutes; let cook with the lid off until the liquid turns into a syrup-like glaze.

7   While the liquid is reducing, rub the meat side of the ribs with the brown sugar and place under the broiler for about 10 minutes, or until golden brown.

8   Pour some of the glaze over the ribs and serve with additional glaze on the side.

Apple Fennel Pork Roast

Just the same as the flavors of sweet Italian sausage, fennel and pork are a match made in heaven to complement this wonderful dish.

Serves 6 to 8

3 pounds boneless pork roast

1½ teaspoons extra-virgin olive oil

1 teaspoon sea kosher salt

½ teaspoon freshly ground black pepper

3 Granny Smith apples, peeled, cored, and sliced

2 fresh figs, halved

1 medium onion, sliced

1 cup chicken stock

¼ cup balsamic vinegar

1 sprig fresh thyme

1 teaspoon cumin seeds

1 teaspoon fennel seeds

1 Preheat the pressure cooker, rub the pork roast with the olive oil, and season with the kosher salt and pepper.

2 Add the roast to the pressure cooker and brown it on all sides.

3 Add the apples, figs, onion, stock, vinegar, thyme, cumin, and fennel to the pressure cooker; secure the lid.

4 When pressure is achieved, set a timer for 25 minutes.

5 When the cook time is complete and pressure is fully released, remove the lid with caution.

6 Remove and discard the thyme.

7 Place the roast on a platter and slice; top with the sauce and serve hot.

Pork Carnitas

Savory pork, fresh tomatoes, garlic, and citrus juices blend to make the perfect pressure cooker creation. Serve with warm tortillas or over rice and beans.

Serves 4 to 6

2 pounds boneless pork shoulder

1 teaspoon kosher salt

½ teaspoon freshly ground black pepper

½ teaspoon ground cumin

1 tablespoon extra-virgin olive oil

½ cup chicken stock

2 tablespoons fresh lemon juice

2 garlic cloves, chopped

1 small onion, diced

2 sliced Serrano chilis, seeds and membrane removed

1 teaspoon chili powder

1 bay leaf

Flour tortillas for serving

Minced onion or cilantro for garnish, if desired

1 Rub the pork with the kosher salt, pepper, and cumin.

2 Heat the olive oil in the pressure cooker, add the pork, and brown well on all sides.

3 Add the stock, lemon juice, garlic, onion, Serranos, chili powder, and bay leaf to the pressure cooker; secure the lid.

4 When pressure is achieved, set a timer for 60 minutes.

5 When the cook time is complete and pressure is fully released, remove the lid with caution.

6 Remove and discard the bay leaf. Serve hot in tortillas with your favorite toppings.

Pork Chops Dijon

Tender, juicy, melt-in-your-mouth pork chops. Add Garlic Mashed Potatoes (page 183), a fresh green salad, and a dry white wine for a spectacular meal anytime.

Serves 4

4 bone-in pork chops, cut into 2-inch slices

½ cup chicken stock

1 tablespoon Dijon mustard

½ cup orange juice

1 teaspoon kosher salt

1 teaspoon freshly ground black pepper

½ cup heavy cream

1   Place the pork chops, stock, mustard, orange juice, kosher salt, and pepper into the pressure cooker; secure the lid.

2   When pressure is achieved, set a timer for 20 minutes.

3   When the cook time is complete and pressure is fully released, remove the lid with caution.

4   Transfer the pork chops to a platter.

5   Stir the cream into liquid remaining in the pressure cooker and cook, stirring until the sauce is smooth. Pour the sauce over the pork chops and serve.

Pork a l'Orange

Your dinner guests will think you slaved all day in the kitchen over this pork dish! The orange-infused pork will melt in your mouth.

Serves 4

1 tablespoon extra-virgin olive oil

4 bone-in pork chops, cut into 1-inch thick slices

½ teaspoon kosher salt

½ teaspoon freshly ground black pepper

½ cup chicken stock

¼ cup brown sugar

1 teaspoon cider vinegar

1 teaspoon freshly grated ginger

½ teaspoon dry mustard

1 teaspoon dried marjoram

1 teaspoon orange zest

1 sprig fresh thyme

2 oranges, peeled and sectioned

1. Preheat the pressure cooker and add the olive oil.

2. Rub the pork chops with the kosher salt and pepper and brown in the pressure cooker on both sides, one at a time. Remove the pork chops from the pressure cooker and set aside on a plate.

3. Add the stock to the pressure cooker to deglaze, scraping up all the little bits from the bottom.

4. Return the pork chops to the pressure cooker. Add the brown sugar, vinegar, ginger, mustard, marjoram, orange zest, thyme, and orange sections to the pressure cooker; secure the lid.

5. When pressure is achieved, set a timer for 20 minutes.

6. When the cook time is complete and pressure is fully released, remove the lid with caution.

7. Remove and discard the thyme and serve immediately.

Hard Cider Pulled Pork

Serve this pulled pork on brioche rolls topped with a creamy coleslaw, and spice it up with a little Sriracha sauce if you like it hot.

Serves 4 to 6

1 tablespoon extra-virgin olive oil

1 Boston butt roast
(3 to 4 pounds)

1 teaspoon kosher salt

1 teaspoon garlic kosher salt

1 teaspoon sweet paprika

1 teaspoon freshly ground
black pepper

One 12-ounce bottle
hard apple cider

½ cup chicken stock

1 cup barbeque sauce

10 brioche sandwich rolls, toasted

1   Preheat the oven to 375°F.

2   Preheat the pressure cooker for 2 minutes.

3   Add the olive oil to the pressure cooker and let heat for 2 minutes.

4   Pat the pork dry, then rub with the kosher salt, garlic kosher salt, paprika, and pepper.

5   Place the pork in the pressure cooker and sear each side well, approximately 5 minutes per side.

6   Add the cider, stock, and barbeque sauce to the pressure cooker; secure the lid.

7   When pressure is achieved, set a timer for 60 minutes.

8   When the cook time is complete and pressure is fully released, remove the lid with caution.

9   Remove the pork to a platter, and turn the pressure cooker back on to reduce the cooking liquid by half while cutting up the pork, discarding any fat.

10 Add the diced pork back into the pot and stir to combine.

11 Serve on the toasted brioche rolls.

Pork with Apples

You can never have enough apples! Serve this dish with a side of sauce for extra goodness. The pork will cut with your fork; the aroma will fill your house.

Serves 4 to 6

2 pounds boneless pork loin

1 teaspoon kosher salt

½ teaspoon freshly ground black pepper

½ teaspoon fennel seeds

1 shallot, chopped

2 large Granny Smith apples, cored and sliced

½ cup chicken stock

½ cup apple cider

1 cinnamon stick

1 Season the pork with kosher salt and pepper.

2 Place the pork, fennel, shallot, apples, stock, cider, and cinnamon stick into the pressure cooker; secure the lid.

3 When pressure is achieved, set a timer for 50 minutes.

4 When the cook time is complete and pressure is fully released, remove the lid with caution.

5 Remove the cinnamon stick.

6 Serve the pork and apples on a platter with a ladle of the cooking liquid.

Cherry Pepper Pork Chops

This meal is perfect with Stuffed Apples (page 265). The recipe serves four, and leftovers are great for next day's lunch.

Serves 4

2 tablespoons extra-virgin olive oil

4 boneless pork chops

One 6-ounce box long grain and wild rice mix, with seasoning packet

One 6-ounce jar sweet cherry peppers, with juice

1 cup chicken stock

1 tablespoon kosher salt

¼ teaspoon freshly ground black pepper

1 Add the olive oil to the pressure cooker and heat for 5 minutes.

2 Add the pork chops to the pressure cooker, two at a time, and cook on both sides for 7 minutes.

3 Add the rice with seasoning packet, cherry peppers, stock, kosher salt, and pepper to the pressure cooker; secure the lid.

4 When pressure is achieved, set a timer for 15 minutes.

5 When the cook time is complete and pressure is fully released, remove the lid with caution.

6 Serve immediately.

Southern Style BBQ Pulled Pork

This pulled pork makes for an incredible sandwich! Top with slaw for ultimate flavor, and if you're feeling extra inspired, hollow out the inside of a corn muffin and fill with this flavorful pulled pork. Pro tip: after assembly, store inside a muffin tin for easy transport and cleanup for parties and tailgates.

Serves 6 to 8

4 pounds boneless pork butt roast

1 teaspoon kosher salt

1 teaspoon garlic kosher salt

1 teaspoon sweet paprika

1 teaspoon freshly ground black pepper

2 teaspoons soy sauce

2 cups apple cider

One 16-ounce bottle barbecue sauce

1 tablespoon cider vinegar

Sandwich rolls for serving

1 Place the pork, kosher salt, garlic kosher salt, paprika, pepper, soy sauce, and cider into the pressure cooker; secure the lid.

2 When pressure is achieved, set a timer for 60 minutes.

3 When the cook time is complete and pressure is fully released, remove the lid with caution.

4 Remove the roast, cut into slices, and return the slices to the pressure cooker.

5 Add the barbecue sauce and vinegar to the pressure cooker; secure the lid.

6 When pressure is achieved, set a timer for 20 minutes.

7 When the cook time is complete and pressure is fully released, remove the lid with caution.

8 Serve on sandwich rolls.

One-Pot Wonders

Scalloped Potatoes with Ham

Creamy, cheesy potatoes with hunks of ham… need I say more?

Serves 6 to 8

2 tablespoons unsalted butter

1 pound ham, cut into 1-inch pieces

1 medium onion, thinly sliced

2 garlic cloves, minced

2½ pounds Russet potatoes, peeled and sliced 1 inch thick

1 tablespoon chopped fresh thyme leaves

1 teaspoon kosher salt

½ teaspoon freshly ground black pepper

½ cup chicken stock

½ cup heavy cream

Pinch of nutmeg

4 ounces grated Cheddar cheese

2 tablespoons chopped fresh chives

1 Place the butter in the pressure cooker and heat with the lid off.

2 When the butter is melted, add the ham and sauté for 4 minutes.

3 Add the onion, garlic, potatoes, thyme, kosher salt, pepper, stock, cream, nutmeg, and cheese to the pressure cooker; secure the lid.

4 When pressure is achieved, set a timer for 15 minutes.

5 When the cook time is complete and pressure is fully released, remove the lid with caution.

6 Let rest for 10 minutes, top with the chives, and serve.

Bacon Tomato Macaroni and Cheese

Kids will love this macaroni and cheese, and so will dad, with the added savory bacon. How easy can dinner be? A fun twist on an old favorite.

Serves 4 to 6

2½ cups dry elbow macaroni

2 cups chicken stock

1 teaspoon kosher salt

1 teaspoon freshly ground black pepper

1 cup heavy cream

1 tablespoon unsalted butter

½ cup whole milk

1½ cups shredded Cheddar cheese

1½ cups shredded mozzarella cheese

6 strips bacon, cooked crisp and crumbled, divided

1 heirloom tomato, seeded and diced

4 green onions, including some of the dark green part, chopped

1 Place the macaroni, stock, kosher salt, and pepper into the pressure cooker; secure the lid.

2 When pressure is achieved, set a timer for 8 minutes.

3 When the cook time is complete and pressure is fully released, remove the lid with caution.

4 Stir in the cream, unsalted butter, and milk.

5 Add the cheeses, half of the bacon, and half of the tomato to the pressure cooker and stir until creamy.

6 Sprinkle the remaining bacon and tomatoes and the green onions on top.

7 Serve immediately.

Lobster Macaroni and Cheese

What could be better than luscious lobster with creamy macaroni and cheese with a crunchy crust! This dish is comfort and luxury all in one.

Serves 4

1 cup chicken stock

1 live Maine lobster (about 1 pound)

1½ cups dry elbow pasta

1 cup heavy cream

¼ cup whipped cream cheese

¼ cup shredded white Vermont Cheddar cheese

¼ cup shredded Fontina cheese

¼ cup shredded Parmesan cheese

Freshly ground black pepper

Pinch of nutmeg

½ cup finely chopped Kettle potato chips

1   Bring the stock to a boil in the pressure cooker.

2   Add the lobster to the pressure cooker, head first; secure the lid.

3   When pressure is achieved, set a timer for 3 minutes.

4   When the cook time is complete and pressure is fully released, remove the lid with caution. Remove the lobster from the pressure cooker and set aside to clean.

5   Add the dry pasta to the pressure cooker; secure the lid.

6   When pressure is achieved, set a timer for 5 minutes.

7   When the cook time is complete and pressure is fully released, remove the lid with caution. Add the cream and stir. Add the cheeses, pepper, and nutmeg and stir until smooth and the cheeses are melted and creamy.

8   Remove the meat from the claws and tail of the lobster. Stir the lobster meat into the pasta.

9   Sprinkle with potato chips.

10 Optional: Transfer the macaroni and cheese to an oven-proof pan and pop under the broiler for 1 to 2 minutes. Serve hot!

Jambalaya

This Louisiana Creole dish is known for its ability to stretch a budget, and now it's saving you time, too. Pressure cooking this classic will infuse every grain of rice with smoky sausage flavor to maximum capacity, without slow-cooking all day. Serve with fresh French bread for an authentic feel.

Serves 6

1 pound Andouille sausage, diced

1 tablespoon extra-virgin olive oil

1 medium onion, diced

4 boneless chicken thighs, cut into 1-inch cubes

½ teaspoon kosher salt

½ teaspoon freshly ground black pepper

1 red bell pepper, diced

2 celery stalks, diced

2 garlic cloves, minced

2 cups dry long-grain rice

½ teaspoon dried thyme

1 teaspoon Cajun seasoning

1 tablespoon hot pepper sauce

1½ cups chicken stock

½ cup crushed tomatoes

1 pound jumbo shrimp, peeled and deveined

4 green onions, chopped

1   Preheat the pressure cooker.

2   Add the sausage and brown on all sides for 3 minutes.

3   Add the olive oil and heat for 1 minutes.

4   Add the onion and cook for 1 minute.

5   Add the chicken thighs, kosher salt, pepper, bell pepper, celery, garlic, rice, thyme, Cajun seasoning, hot pepper sauce, stock, and tomatoes to the pressure cooker; stir well and secure the lid.

6   When pressure is achieved, set a timer for 6 minutes.

7   When the cook time is complete and pressure is fully released, remove the lid with caution.

8   Stir in the shrimp and green onions.

9   Secure the lid and let the shrimp cook in the hot rice for 5 minutes without turning on the pressure cooker.

10 Serve hot.

Paella

This traditional Spanish dish is easy to make at home. The medley of meats gives it its famous heartiness. A real taste of Spain in minutes.

Serves 6

4 small bone-in chicken thighs

1 tablespoon extra-virgin olive oil

½ teaspoon kosher salt

¼ teaspoon freshly ground black pepper

1 shallot, chopped

3 garlic cloves, minced

1 red bell pepper, cored and diced

¼ teaspoon saffron strands

½ pound chorizo, sliced

1 tablespoon tomato paste

2 cups dry Arborio rice

2½ cups chicken stock

1 pound large shrimp, peeled and deveined

1 pound mussels, debearded

½ cup frozen baby peas, thawed

2 tablespoons sliced stuffed olives

1 Preheat the pressure cooker. Rub the chicken thighs with the olive oil and season with kosher salt and pepper.

2 Add the chicken to the pressure cooker and brown well on all sides.

3 Add the shallot and cook for 1 minute.

4 Add the garlic, bell pepper, saffron, and chorizo and brown for 2 minutes longer.

5 Add the tomato paste, rice, and stock. Stir well, then secure the pressure cooker lid.

6 When pressure is achieved, set a timer for 6 minutes.

7 When the cook time is complete and pressure is fully released, remove the lid with caution.

8 Stir in the shrimp and mussels and quickly secure the lid. Let the pressure cooker sit for several minutes with the lid on to cook the shellfish through.

9 Spoon the paella onto a serving platter and sprinkle with the peas and olives.

10 Serve hot.

Shepherd's Pie

Everybody's favorite comfort food. What's better than meat in a creamy gravy with mashed potatoes on top? Make extra to freeze for the nights the babysitter is watching the kids.

Serves 4 to 6

1 tablespoon extra-virgin olive oil

1½ pounds ground beef or lamb

1 cup diced onion

2 celery stalks, chopped

2 carrots, peeled and diced

2 garlic cloves, minced

1 teaspoon kosher salt

½ teaspoon freshly ground black pepper

2 teaspoons tomato paste

½ cup beef stock

1 teaspoon Worcestershire sauce

1 sprig fresh thyme

1 sprig fresh rosemary

1 tablespoon gravy flour, dissolved in 1 tablespoon water

½ cup fresh or frozen baby peas

½ cup fresh or frozen corn kernels

4 cups fresh or frozen mashed potatoes

½ teaspoon sweet paprika

1. Preheat the pressure cooker for 2 minutes. Add the olive oil and heat for 2 minutes.

2. Add the ground meat and cook, breaking up with a wooden spoon while cooking.

3. Drain the fat from the meat by removing the insert and straining the meat through a colander; set aside.

4. Add the onion and cook for 2 minutes, stirring occasionally.

5. Add the celery, carrots, and garlic and cook until tender, about 5 minutes.

6. Return the meat to the pressure cooker, along with the kosher salt, pepper, and tomato paste, and cook for 1 minute.

7. Add the stock, Worcestershire sauce, thyme, and rosemary to the pressure cooker; secure the lid.

8. When pressure is achieved, set a timer for 10 minutes.

9. When the cook time is complete and pressure is fully released, remove the lid with caution.

10. Remove and discard the thyme and rosemary.

11. Stir the dissolved gravy flour into the meat mixture.

12. Top with peas and corn, then spread the mashed potatoes evenly over the top; secure the pressure cooker lid.

13. When pressure is achieved, set a timer for 5 minutes.

14. When the cook time is complete and pressure is fully released, remove the lid with caution.

15. Sprinkle with paprika and serve immediately.

Tuna Casserole

Truly a low-budget meal, but no one can deny they love this dish.

Serves 8

12 ounces dry egg noodles

4 cups chicken stock

1 medium onion, chopped

1 red bell pepper, chopped

10 ounces button mushrooms, sliced

3 cups half-and-half

1 (10.5-ounce) can condensed cream of celery soup

3 (5-ounce) cans water-packed albacore tuna, drained

1 cup shredded Monterey Jack cheese

1 cup shredded sharp Cheddar cheese

1 teaspoon kosher salt

½ teaspoon freshly ground black pepper

1 cup crushed potato chips

1   Place the egg noodles, stock, onion, bell pepper, and mushrooms into the pressure cooker; secure the lid.

2   When pressure is achieved, set a timer for 8 minutes.

3   When cook time is complete and pressure is fully released, remove the lid with caution.

4   Stir in the half-and-half, cream of celery soup, tune, cheeses, kosher salt, and pepper.

5   Top with the crushed potato chips and serve.

Beef and Rice with Broccoli

Veggies don't have to be boring with this beef, broccoli, and rice combo.

Serves 4 to 6

1 tablespoon extra-virgin olive oil

2 pounds round steak, cut into 1-inch pieces

1 medium onion, thinly sliced

2 garlic cloves, minced

1 cup basmati rice, rinsed and drained

2 cups beef stock

¼ teaspoon kosher salt

¼ teaspoon freshly ground black pepper

2 cups coarsely chopped broccoli florets

1   Preheat the olive oil in the pressure cooker; add the meat and brown on all sides.

2   Add the onion and garlic and cook for 5 minutes.

3   Add the rice and stir to coat, about 1 minute more.

4   Pour the beef stock, kosher salt, and black pepper into the pressure cooker and stir; secure the lid.

5   When pressure is achieved, set a timer for 10 minutes.

6   When the cook time is complete and pressure is fully released, remove the lid with caution.

7   Add the broccoli to the pressure cooker, close the lid, and let rest for 1 minute.

8   Serve immediately.

Cheesy Lasagna

This quick Sunday dinner does double-duty as leftovers. Freeze it for a fresh meal next week.

Serves 12

1 tablespoon extra virgin olive oil

1 medium onion, diced

1 pound ground beef

¼ teaspoon sea kosher salt

¼ teaspoon freshly ground black pepper

One 24-ounce jar pasta sauce

¼ cup water

2 pounds ricotta cheese

1 package frozen spinach, thawed and drained well

2 large eggs

⅓ cup grated Parmesan cheese

2 teaspoons minced garlic

1½ cups mozzarella cheese, shredded

1 teaspoon Italian seasoning

¼ teaspoons red pepper flakes

8 ounces no-boil lasagna noodles

1   Preheat the oil in the pressure cooker and add the onion, ground beef, kosher salt, and pepper.

2   Cook until the onion is slightly soft and the beef is browned, using a wooden spoon to break up the meat.

3   Strain the meat to remove excess fat.

4   In a large bowl, add the cooked meat, pasta sauce, and water and stir.

5   In another bowl, combine the ricotta, spinach, eggs, Parmesan cheese, garlic, and two-thirds of the mozzarella, Italian seasoning, kosher salt, and pepper.

6   Spray the pressure cooker with nonstick cooking spray.

7   Using a ladle, layer one-fifth of the beef and sauce into the bottom of the pressure cooker, then top with a layer of noodles.

8   Cover the noodles with one-quarter of the cheese mixture.

9   Repeat until all of the layers are used, ending with a layer of noodles topped with sauce. Secure the pressure cooker lid.

10 When pressure is achieved, set a timer for 10 minutes.

11 When the cook time is complete and pressure is fully released, allow it to rest for 10 minutes, covered. Remove the lid with caution and serve warm.

6 min.

Bow Tie Carbonara

This no-brainer recipe is an easy Italian favorite for those nights when you want a taste of Italy at home.

Serves 2 to 4

1 pound dry bow tie pasta

¼ teaspoon coarse freshly ground black pepper

3 cups chicken stock

1 cup light cream

½ cup grated Parmesan or Romano cheese

1 large egg, beaten

2 tablespoons unsalted butter

¼ cup chopped fresh parsley

6 slices bacon, cooked crisp and crumbled

1   Add the pasta, black pepper, and chicken stock to the pressure cooker; secure the lid.

2   When pressure is achieved, set a timer for 6 minutes.

3   When the cook time is complete and pressure is fully released, remove the lid with caution.

4   Stir in the light cream, then add the cheese and mix until smooth.

5   Stir in the egg and butter, and top with the parsley and bacon, and serve.

Buffalo Chicken Macaroni and Cheese

The kids will love this combo! The creamy cheese offsets the spice in this dish, but there's still some kick nonetheless.

Serves 4 to 6

6 chicken tenders

1 pound dry rigatoni pasta

4 cups chicken stock

1 small onion, chopped

2 celery stalks, chopped

1 large carrot, peeled and chopped

⅔ cup buffalo wing sauce

1 tablespoon ranch seasoning (optional)

½ cup cream cheese

½ cup half-and-half

1 cup shredded sharp Cheddar cheese

1 cup shredded Swiss cheese

½ cup crumbled Gorgonzola cheese, divided

1 cup crushed cheddar-flavored French fried onions

1   Place the chicken, pasta, stock, onion, celery, carrot, wing sauce, and ranch seasoning into the pressure cooker; secure the lid.

2   When pressure is achieved, set a timer for 10 minutes.

3   When the cook time is complete and pressure is fully released, remove the lid with caution.

4   Add the cream cheese to the pressure cooker and stir until dissolved.

5   Add the half-and-half, Cheddar cheese, Swiss cheese, and ¼ cup of the Gorgonzola cheese to the pressure cooker; stir until dissolved.

6   Top with the French fried onions and remaining Gorgonzola and serve.

Cheesy Potato with Ham and Spinach

This is a great time to use that leftover Easter ham. Creamy, cheesy potato and ham goodness.

Serves 6 to 8

1 tablespoon unsalted butter

8 ounces baby spinach

3 garlic cloves, minced

½ cup heavy cream

1 cup chicken stock

1 cup grated Parmesan cheese

1 teaspoon kosher salt

1 teaspoon white pepper

⅛ teaspoon nutmeg

4 ounces sliced Black Forest ham, diced

2 pounds Yukon Gold potatoes, peeled and sliced ⅛ inch thick

2 tablespoons chopped fresh chives

1 Preheat the unsalted butter in the pressure cooker; add the spinach and garlic, and sauté for 4 minutes.

2 Add the cream, stock, Parmesan cheese, kosher salt, white pepper, nutmeg, ham, and potatoes to the pressure cooker; stir, then secure the lid.

3 When pressure is achieved, set a timer for 5 minutes.

4 When the cook time is complete and pressure is fully released, remove the lid with caution.

5 Serve immediately, garnished with the chives.

25 min.

Chicken and Sweet Potato Dumplings

A twist on the classic, the sweet potatoes in this version offer a healthier alternative to the traditional dumplings. Could be your new favorite.

Serves 6

6 bone-in, skinless chicken thighs

2 teaspoons kosher salt, divided

1 teaspoon freshly ground black pepper

½ teaspoon chopped fresh rosemary leaves

1 tablespoon extra-virgin olive oil

¼ cup white wine

1 cup chicken stock

½ cup pearl onions

1 celery stalk, sliced

1 large carrot, peeled and sliced

1 sprig fresh thyme

1½ cups buttermilk

1¼ cups unbleached flour

1 cup mashed sweet potatoes

2 teaspoons baking powder

¼ cup frozen baby peas

1   Season both sides of the chicken with 1 teaspoon of the kosher salt, the pepper, and rosemary.

2   Preheat the olive oil in the pressure cooker over medium heat.

3   Add the chicken to the pan; brown for 3 minutes on each side.

4   Add the wine and stock to the pan to deglaze; scrape up all the little bits from the bottom.

5   Add the onions, celery, carrot, and thyme, to the pressure cooker; secure the lid.

6   When pressure is achieved, set a timer for 25 minutes.

7   While the chicken is cooking, combine the buttermilk, flour, sweet potatoes, and baking powder in a bowl; mix well.

8   When the cook time is complete and pressure is fully released, remove the lid with caution.

9   Remove and discard the thyme.

10 With the lid off, turn on the pressure cooker. When the contents are simmering, drop the sweet potato dumpling mixture by the spoonful into the pressure cooker.

11 Cook the dumplings for 3 minutes on each side, and add the peas before serving.

Greek Lemon Chicken and Rice

This dish brings the tastes and smells of the Mediterranean to your home for a quick meal everyone will love. Serve with a chilled cucumber and tomato salad drizzled with extra-virgin olive oil.

Serves 4

2 boneless, skinless chicken breasts, cubed

1 teaspoon extra-virgin olive oil

4 bone-in chicken thighs, trimmed of fat

1 medium onion, diced

4 garlic cloves, minced

1 teaspoon lemon zest

4 tablespoons fresh lemon juice

1 tablespoon dried oregano

¼ teaspoon dried thyme

1 cup dry basmati rice, rinsed

1 cup chicken stock

2 teaspoons kosher salt

2 teaspoons freshly ground black pepper

1 Heat the oil in the pressure cooker with lid off; add the chicken and brown well on both sides.

2 Add the onion and garlic and cook for an additional 1 minute.

3 Add the lemon zest, lemon juice, oregano, thyme, rice, stock, kosher salt, and pepper to the pressure cooker; secure the lid.

4 When pressure is achieved, set a timer for 8 minutes.

5 When the cook time is complete and pressure is fully released, remove the lid with caution.

6 Stir and serve.

Chicken and Yellow Rice

Rich chicken-flavored rice in half the time.
A full, satisfying meal all in one pan, which
makes cleanup a snap.

Serves 4 to 6

1 tablespoon extra-virgin olive oil

1 teaspoon kosher salt

½ teaspoon freshly ground
black pepper

One 16-ounce bag dry yellow rice

2 cups water

1 tablespoon chopped pimentos

½ cup Spanish olives

1 cup frozen peas

1   Preheat the pressure cooker, add the olive oil,
and heat for 2 minutes.

2   Season the chicken with kosher salt and pepper
and add to the pressure cooker.

3   When the chicken has browned well, add the rice,
water, and pimentos to the pressure cooker;
secure the lid.

4   When pressure is achieved, set a timer for 8 minutes.

5   When the cook time is complete and pressure is fully
released, stir in the olives and peas and serve.

Chicken Enchilada Casserole

All of your favorite Mexican flavors in one easy dish.
Creamy and cheesy, with just the right amount of heat.

Serves 4 to 6

2 pounds boneless, skinless chicken breasts

1 (4-ounce) can green chilis, chopped

1 (1-ounce) envelope taco seasoning

1 cup chicken stock

2 cups corn tortilla chips

1 (10-ounce) can enchilada sauce

1 cup grated Colby and Cheddar cheese blend

3 green onions, chopped

Sour cream for garnish

1   Place the chicken, chilis, taco seasoning, and stock into the pressure cooker; secure the lid.

2   When pressure is achieved, set a timer for 15 minutes.

3   When the cook time is complete and pressure is fully released, open the lid with caution.

4   Add the tortilla chips, enchilada sauce, and cheese to the pressure cooker; stir, then secure the lid.

5   When pressure is achieved, set a timer for 3 minutes.

6   When the cook time is complete and pressure is fully released, remove the lid with caution.

7   Garnish with the green onions and sour cream, and serve immediately.

Chicken with Mushroom Orzo

Tender chicken with tomatoes and vegetables complements this tiny pasta with Mediterranean flavors.

Serves 6

1½ teaspoons extra-virgin olive oil

2 boneless, skinless chicken breasts, chopped into 1 inch pieces

½ teaspoon kosher salt

¼ teaspoon freshly ground black pepper

1 small onion, thinly sliced

2 cups sliced baby Portobello mushrooms

2 garlic cloves, minced

1 cup dry orzo

2 Roma tomatoes, seeded and chopped

One 14.5-ounce can chicken stock

2 medium zucchini, cut into ½-inch pieces

2 teaspoons chopped fresh thyme

1 Preheat the pressure cooker and heat the olive oil for 2 minutes.

2 Add the chicken and brown on all sides.

3 Season with kosher salt and pepper and add the onion, mushrooms, and garlic to the pressure cooker; cook for 5 minutes.

4 Stir in the orzo and cook for an additional minute.

5 Pour the tomatoes and stock into the pressure cooker; secure the lid.

6 When pressure is achieved, set a timer for 8 minutes.

7 When the cook time is complete and pressure is fully released, remove the lid with caution.

8 Add the zucchini and thyme, and cook with the lid off for 5 to 7 minutes, until the vegetables are softened.

9 Serve warm.

8 min.

Creamy Tomato Beef Noodles

This tender beef in a creamy tomato sauce packs noodles with flavor. A real old-fashioned, feel-good food.

Serves 4 to 6

1 teaspoon extra-virgin olive oil

1 pound lean ground beef

2 (8-ounce) cans tomato sauce

1 teaspoon dried basil

¼ teaspoon red pepper flakes

½ teaspoon sugar

½ teaspoon garlic powder

¼ teaspoon sea kosher salt

¼ teaspoon freshly ground black pepper

1 cup beef stock

2 cups dry egg noodles

1 cup plain Greek yogurt

One 8-ounce package cream cheese, softened

½ cup whole milk

1 (10-ounce) package frozen spinach, well drained

½ cup shredded Cheddar cheese

1 Heat the olive oil in the pressure cooker with the lid off; add the beef and cook until browned, breaking up the meat with a wooden spoon .

2 Drain off the fat and stir in the tomato sauce, basil, red pepper flakes, sugar, garlic powder, kosher salt, black pepper, stock, and noodles; secure the pressure cooker lid.

3 When pressure is achieved, set a timer for 8 minutes.

4 Meanwhile, in a medium bowl, combine the yogurt and cream cheese and process with an electric blender until smooth; stir in the milk.

5 Stir in the spinach and Cheddar cheese.

6 When the cook time is complete and pressure is fully released, remove the lid with caution.

7 Stir the yogurt mixture into the beef.

8 Serve immediately.

8 min.

Macaroni and Cheese

Macaroni and cheese is the ultimate comfort food and a favorite among kids. They will love the creaminess and you will love the ease!

Serves 4 to 6

2½ cups dry elbow macaroni

2 cups chicken stock

½ cup heavy cream

1 teaspoon kosher salt

1 teaspoon freshly ground black pepper

1 tablespoon unsalted butter

½ cup whole milk

1½ cups shredded Cheddar cheese

1½ cups shredded mozzarella cheese

½ teaspoon dry mustard

2 large eggs, beaten

1 Place the macaroni, stock, cream, kosher salt, and pepper into the pressure cooker; secure the lid.

2 When pressure is achieved, set a timer for 8 minutes.

3 When the cook time is complete and pressure is fully released, remove the lid with caution.

4 Add the unsalted butter, milk, cheeses, mustard, and eggs to the pressure cooker and stir until creamy.

5 Serve immediately.

Burgundy Meatballs and Noodles

This dish offers rich, beefy flavor, and the Burgundy wine gives it that extra-special flavor. Serve over noodles, or as a snack at your next cocktail party.

Serves 6 to 8

2 cups beef stock

Two 1-ounce packages beef gravy mix

30 small fully cooked meatballs

2 cups chopped onions

1 cup Burgundy wine

¼ cup ketchup

1 sprig fresh thyme

3 cups cooked egg noodles for serving

1   Heat the stock in the pressure cooker, add the gravy mix, and stir to dissolve.

2   Add the meatballs, onions, wine, ketchup, and thyme to the pressure cooker; secure the lid.

3   When pressure is achieved, set a timer for 8 minutes.

4   When the cook time is complete and pressure is fully released, remove the lid with caution.

5   Remove and discard the thyme and serve the meatballs over egg noodles.

Teriyaki Chicken and Rice

An Asian favorite, Teriyaki Chicken and Rice is even better when served with your favorite stir-fry veggies.

Serves 4

1 tablespoon extra-virgin olive oil

4 bone-in chicken thighs, trimmed of fat

½ teaspoon sea kosher salt

¼ teaspoon freshly ground black pepper

3 garlic cloves, minced

¼ cup teriyaki sauce

1½ cups chicken stock, divided

¼ cup cider vinegar

¼ cup honey

½ teaspoon Sriracha

1 cup dry basmati rice, rinsed

5 green onions, sliced

½ cup chopped pineapple

1   Heat the olive oil in the pressure cooker with the lid off.

2   Season the chicken with kosher salt and pepper, add to the pressure cooker with the garlic, and brown well on both sides.

3   Add the teriyaki sauce, ½ cup of the stock, the vinegar, honey, and Sriracha to the pressure cooker; secure the lid.

4   When pressure is achieved, set a timer for 5 minutes.

5   When the cook time is complete and pressure is fully released, remove the lid with caution.

6   Add the rice and remaining 1 cup stock to the pressure cooker; secure the lid.

7   When pressure is achieved, set a timer for 8 minutes.

8   When the cook time is complete and pressure is fully released, remove the lid with caution.

9   Sprinkle with the green onions and pineapple and serve.

Unstuffed Cabbage

These cabbage rolls are stuffed with a mixture of savory ground pork and chuck and creamy cheese.

Serves 4

1 pound ground chuck

½ cup dry white rice

1 teaspoon kosher salt

½ teaspoon freshly ground black pepper

8 large cabbage leaves

1 (15-ounce) can tomato sauce

1½ cups beef stock

1 cup grated Swiss cheese

1 teaspoon dried oregano

1 small onion, chopped

½ teaspoon thyme leaves

½ teaspoon garlic powder

1   In a large bowl, add the meat, rice, kosher salt, and pepper; mix well and divide into four equal portions.

2   Place 2 leaves of cabbage on the bottom of the pressure cooker pan, crumble one portion of the meat mixture on top, and then repeat with three more layers of cabbage leaves and meat. Pour in the tomato sauce, stock, onion, thyme, and garlic powder. Top with cheese, and oregano; secure the pressure cooker lid.

3   When pressure is achieved, set a timer for 15 minutes.

4   When the cook time is complete and pressure is fully released, remove the lid with caution.

5   Serve immediately.

Freezer-Pantry Pasta

No thawing needed here. Now you have no excuse not to cook! Throw it all in, pour yourself a glass of wine, and relax while dinner cooks itself.

Serves 4 to 6

1 pound frozen ground beef

3 cups dry penne or ziti pasta

2½ cups beef stock

3 cups pasta sauce

1 teaspoon kosher salt

½ teaspoon freshly ground black pepper

1 teaspoon Italian seasoning

½ teaspoon garlic powder

½ cup shredded mozzarella cheese

1 Place all of the ingredients into the pressure cooker in the order in which they are listed; secure the lid.

2 When pressure is achieved, set a timer for 20 minutes.

3 When the cook time is complete and pressure is fully released, remove the lid with caution.

4 Break the meat apart using a rubber spatula, stir, and serve.

Mediterranean Chicken with Spinach and Artichokes

This light dish won't leave you feeling bogged down. The nutrients are kept in the spinach and artichokes by the pressure cooking.

Serves 4

1 tablespoon extra-virgin olive oil

4 bone-in chicken thighs

¼ teaspoon kosher salt

¼ teaspoon freshly ground black pepper

1 (14.5-ounce) can artichoke hearts, rinsed and drained

1 medium onion, sliced

1 large carrot, peeled and cut into 1-inch pieces

2 garlic cloves, minced

8 ounces baby spinach

½ cup chicken stock

1 Preheat the olive oil in the pressure cooker with the lid off.

2 Season the chicken with kosher salt and pepper and add to the pressure cooker.

3 Brown the chicken on both sides, about 5 minutes per side; remove and set aside.

4 Add the artichokes, onion, carrot, and garlic to the pressure cooker; cook for 5 minutes.

5 Add the spinach and cook for an additional minute.

6 Add the stock and chicken to the pressure cooker; secure the lid.

7 When pressure is achieved, set a timer for 10 minutes.

8 When the cook time is complete and pressure is fully released, remove the lid with caution.

9 Serve immediately.

Mushroom Spinach Lasagna

A lasagna to get any veggie-lover's mouth to water! Mushrooms bring much-needed protein, and spinach is swirled in with the cheese.

Serves 4 to 6

1 tablespoon extra-virgin olive oil

8 ounces baby Portobello mushrooms, sliced

1 pound baby spinach

2 garlic cloves, minced

1 small onion, diced

½ teaspoon dried oregano

1 teaspoon sea kosher salt

1 teaspoon freshly ground black pepper

2 large eggs, beaten

2 cups whole-milk ricotta cheese

1 pound mozzarella cheese, shredded

1 teaspoon fresh basil, torn

9 ounces dry no-boil lasagna pasta

1 cup chicken stock

1 Heat the olive oil in the pressure cooker with the lid off; add the mushrooms, spinach, garlic, onion, oregano, kosher salt, and pepper; sauté for 5 minutes. Remove the vegetable mixture to a bowl.

2 In a medium bowl, combine the eggs, ricotta, mozzarella, and basil.

3 Spray the pan of the pressure cooker with nonstick cooking spray and start layering your ingredients in the pressure cooker, starting with a layer of the vegetable mixture, followed by the cheese mixture, then the pasta, and repeat. Pour the stock into the pressure cooker; secure the lid.

4 When pressure is achieved, set a timer for 15 minutes.

5 When the cook time is complete and pressure is fully released, remove the lid with caution.

6 Serve immediately.

Gnocchi with Sausage and Kale

These decadent gnocchi are infused with sausage flavor and topped with kale. A nice treat for an otherwise uneventful day.

Serves 4

1 tablespoon extra-virgin olive oil

1½ pounds sweet Italian sausage, casings removed

5 cups stemmed, chopped kale

1 pound baby Portobello mushrooms, sliced

½ cup sun-dried tomatoes

2 garlic cloves, minced

¼ teaspoon red pepper flakes

¼ teaspoons sea kosher salt

¼ teaspoon freshly ground black pepper

1 teaspoon dried basil

1½ cups chicken stock

1 pound cooked gnocchi for serving

1 cup grated Parmesan cheese

1   Preheat the olive oil in the pressure cooker with the lid off.

2   Add the sausage and sauté until cooked through, then drain off excess fat.

3   Add the kale, mushrooms, sun-dried tomatoes, garlic, red pepper flakes, kosher salt, pepper, and basil; sauté 5 minutes.

4   Pour the stock into the pressure cooker; secure the lid.

5   When pressure is achieved, set a timer for 5 minutes.

6   When the cook time is complete and pressure is fully released, remove the lid with caution.

7   Stir in the gnocchi and cheese; heat through. Serve hot.

Pasta with Beans, Chard, and Rosemary

This one-pot wonder is the perfect light and savory meal. Serve it as a side dish or with a crisp salad as a meal.

Serves 4 to 6

3 ounces pancetta, diced

1 medium onion, diced

12 ounces Swiss chard, leaves coarsely chopped, stems finely chopped

¼ teaspoon dried thyme

1 teaspoon minced fresh rosemary

1 garlic clove, minced

¼ teaspoon red pepper flakes

1 (15-ounce) can cannellini beans, un-drained

8 ounces dry fusilli pasta

1½ cups vegetable stock

1 cup grated Parmesan cheese

1 tablespoon balsamic vinegar

1 teaspoon kosher salt

1 Preheat the pressure cooker with the lid off.

2 Add the pancetta and sauté until brown.

3 Stir in the onion and chard and cook, stirring occasionally, until slightly softened.

4 Add the thyme, rosemary, garlic, and red pepper flakes, and cook an additional minute.

5 Add the beans with their liquid, pasta, and stock to the pressure cooker; secure the lid.

6 When pressure is achieved, set a timer for 5 minutes.

7 When the cook time is complete and pressure is fully released, remove the lid with caution.

8 Sprinkle with cheese, vinegar, and kosher salt to taste.

9 Serve immediately.

Red Beans with Rice

This hearty rice and beans dish brings smoky sausage flavor to every grain of rice. An all-in-one dish sure to please everyone.

Serves 4 to 6

1 pound dried red kidney beans, rinsed

1 large onion, diced

1 large bell pepper, diced

4 garlic cloves, minced

1 large smoked ham hock

1½ pounds mild smoked sausage, sliced

2 teaspoons chopped fresh thyme

2 bay leaves

2 tablespoons chopped fresh parsley

½ teaspoon kosher salt

½ teaspoon freshly ground black pepper

½ teaspoon cayenne pepper

1 tablespoon hot sauce

1 teaspoon Worcestershire sauce

8 cups chicken stock

4 cups cooked rice for serving

1 Place the beans, onion, bell pepper, garlic, ham hock, sausage, thyme, bay leaves, parsley, kosher salt, pepper, cayenne, hot sauce, Worcestershire sauce, and stock into the pressure cooker; secure the lid.

2 When pressure is achieved, set a timer for 30 minutes.

3 When the cook time is complete and pressure is fully released, remove the lid with caution.

4 Remove and discard the bay leaves, and serve over rice.

Rigatoni with Hot Italian Sausage

Serve this cheesy rigatoni with your favorite Texas toast or cheesy garlic bread. Just enough spice, and plenty of cheese.

Serves 4 to 6

1½ pounds hot Italian sausage in casings

½ cup water

2 cups dry rigatoni pasta

3 cups chicken stock

3 cups pasta sauce

2 cups whole-milk ricotta cheese

2 cups shredded mozzarella cheese

1 teaspoon garlic powder

1 teaspoon kosher salt

1 teaspoon freshly ground black pepper

1 Place the sausage and water into the pressure cooker; secure the lid.

2 When pressure is achieved, set a timer for 10 minutes.

3 When the cook time is complete and pressure is fully released, remove the lid with caution.

4 Remove the sausage and drain the excess liquid.

5 Slice the sausage and return to the pressure cooker.

6 Add the pasta, stock, pasta sauce, cheeses, garlic powder, kosher salt, and pepper to the pressure cooker; secure the lid.

7 When pressure is achieved, set a timer for 12 minutes.

8 When the cook time is complete and pressure is fully released, remove the lid with caution.

9 Serve immediately.

Pork Ribs with Sauerkraut

The sauerkraut is mellowed by the pork in this medley. It suits the sauerkraut diehards, as well as those who are just getting used to the taste.

Serves 4

1 tablespoon extra-virgin olive oil

4 bone-in country-style ribs

1 teaspoon kosher salt

1 teaspoon freshly ground black pepper

One 1-pound jar sauerkraut, drained

1 medium onion, diced

3 garlic cloves, minced

2 carrots, peeled and cut into 1-inch pieces

4 red bliss potatoes, quartered

1 Granny Smith apple, peeled, cored, seeded, and cut into quarters

1   Heat the olive oil in the pressure cooker with the lid off.

2   Season the ribs with kosher salt and pepper, then brown on all sides in the pressure cooker for 2-3 minutes per side.

3   Add the sauerkraut, onion, garlic, carrots, potatoes, and apple to the pressure cooker; secure the lid.

4   When pressure is achieved, set a timer for 20 minutes.

5   When the cook time is complete and pressure is fully released, remove the lid with caution.

6   Serve immediately.

25 min.

Manicotti

Literally meaning "little sleeves" in Italian, this manicotti holds the cheese and filling in place, just like an Italian burrito.

Serves 4 to 6

1 pound ground beef

2 (24-ounce) jars pasta sauce

1 (14.5-ounce) can diced tomatoes

2 teaspoons Italian seasoning

¼ teaspoon sea kosher salt

¼ teaspoon freshly ground black pepper

¼ teaspoon red pepper flakes

2¼ cups whole-milk ricotta cheese

2 cups shredded mozzarella cheese, divided

1¼ cups grated Parmesan cheese

8 ounces dry manicotti shells

1 cup chicken stock

1 Preheat the pressure cooker, add the beef, and cook for 5 minutes, breaking up the meat with a wooden spoon.

2 Pour off excess fat.

3 Add the pasta sauce, diced tomatoes, Italian seasoning, kosher salt, black pepper, and red pepper flakes to the pressure cooker; secure the lid.

4 When pressure is achieved, set a timer for 15 minutes.

5 Meanwhile, in a medium bowl, combine the ricotta, 1 cup of the mozzarella, and the Parmesan cheese.

6 Spoon the cheese mixture into a zip-top bag and snip off a corner.

7 When the cook time is complete and pressure is fully released, remove the lid with caution.

8 Transfer the meat mixture to a separate large bowl.

9 Pipe the cheese mixture into the manicotti shells and place into the pressure cooker.

10 Spoon the meat mixture and pour the stock over the manicotti and top with the remaining 1 cup mozzarella; secure the pressure cooker lid.

11 When pressure is achieved, set a timer for 10 minutes.

12 When the cook time is complete and pressure is fully released, remove the lid with caution.

13 Serve immediately.

10 min.

Ravioli with Meatballs

There's nothing better than little pockets filled with cheese and meatballs bursting with flavor. Serve with your favorite Italian bread, and enjoy!

Serves 4

8 ounces frozen mini meatballs

2 cups beef stock

1 small onion, chopped

2 garlic cloves, minced

½ teaspoon Italian seasoning

1 pound frozen ravioli

1 cup shredded mozzarella cheese

One 28-ounce jar pasta sauce

1   Place the meatballs, stock, onion, garlic, and Italian seasoning into the pressure cooker; secure the lid.

2   When pressure is achieved, set a timer for 8 minutes.

3   When the cook time is complete and pressure is fully released, remove the lid with caution.

4   Stir in the ravioli, cheese, and pasta sauce into the pressure cooker; secure the lid.

5   When pressure is achieved, set a timer for 2 minutes.

6   When the cook time is complete and pressure is fully released, remove the lid with caution.

7   Serve immediately.

Ziti with Fresh Tomato and Basil

I'm talking more than cheese and noodles here; the fresh tomato and basil takes this ziti to a different level. Great for a meatless meal.

Serves 4 to 6

4 cups chicken stock

1 pound dry ziti pasta

1 small onion, chopped

2 garlic cloves, minced

3 pounds fresh ripe tomatoes, peeled, seeded, and chopped

One 14.5-ounce can crushed tomatoes

2 tablespoons heavy cream, optional

¼ cup grated Parmesan cheese

¼ cup fresh pesto

1   Place the stock, pasta, onion, garlic, fresh tomatoes, and canned tomatoes into the pressure cooker; stir, then secure the lid.

2   When pressure is achieved, set a timer for 8 minutes.

3   When the cook time is complete and pressure is fully released, remove the lid with caution.

4   Stir in the cream, then add the cheese and stir until creamy.

5   Stir in the pesto and serve.

Spicy Sausage and Rice

In the days of old, we needed to stretch the family budget. This meal not only will do that, but will bring everyone back for more.

Serves 4 to 6

1 tablespoon extra-virgin olive oil

1 medium onion, diced

1 red bell pepper, diced

3 garlic cloves, minced

2 tablespoons tomato paste

1 teaspoon kosher salt

½ teaspoon cayenne pepper

1 teaspoon ground cumin

1 tablespoon hot Hungarian paprika

½ teaspoon freshly ground black pepper

1 pound smoked sausage, thinly sliced

½ teaspoon dried marjoram

2 cups dry long-grain rice, rinsed

4 cups beef stock

1   Pour the oil into the pressure cooker and let it preheat with the lid off.

2   Add the onion to the pressure cooker and cook for 2 minutes, stirring occasionally.

3   Add the bell pepper and garlic to the pressure cooker; stir.

4   Add the tomato paste to the pressure cooker and cook for an additional 2 minutes.

5   Add the kosher salt, cayenne, cumin, paprika, pepper, sausage, marjoram, rice, and stock to the pressure cooker; secure the lid.

6   When pressure is achieved, set a timer for 6 minutes.

7   When the cook time is complete and pressure is fully released, remove the lid with caution.

8   Stir and serve immediately.

Side Dishes

Delicious Swiss Chard

Top with grilled chicken or salmon, and then drizzle with extra-virgin olive oil and a touch of vinegar, for a light and nourishing meal.

Serves 2 to 4

2 bunches Swiss chard, leaves and stems chopped into 2-inch pieces

½ cup water

1 teaspoon kosher salt

1 teaspoon cider vinegar

1   Place all of the ingredients into the pressure cooker; secure the lid.

2   When pressure is achieved, set a timer for 5 minutes.

3   When the cook time is complete and pressure is fully released, remove the lid with caution.

4   Serve immediately.

Jersey Potato Salad

This delicious potato salad is sure to enhance any BBQ or picnic.

Serves 4 to 6

3 large eggs

2 pounds fingerling potatoes

2 teaspoons dill pickle juice

½ medium onion, finely diced

2 stalks celery, finely diced

Kosher salt

Freshly ground black pepper

½ cup mayonnaise

1   Place the eggs into the pressure cooker and pour in water to cover; secure the lid.

2   When pressure is achieved, set a timer for 8 minutes.

3   When the cook time is complete and pressure is fully released, open the lid with caution.

4   Remove the eggs to an ice bath, let chill, and peel.

5   Pour out the water and add the potatoes to the pressure cooker with just enough water to cover; secure the lid.

6   When pressure is achieved, set a timer for 5 minutes.

7   When the cook time is complete and pressure is fully released, open the lid with caution.

8   Drain the potatoes in a colander, place in a medium bowl, drizzle with the pickle juice, and toss to coat.

9   When the potatoes are cool enough to handle, cut them into ⅛-inch slices.

10   Chop 2 of the hard-boiled eggs and add to the potatoes. Add the onion, celery, kosher salt, and pepper and toss to combine.

11   Add the mayonnaise and mix thoroughly. Slice the remaining hard-boiled egg and use it to garnish the salad.

Balsamic Beets

Delicious paired with feta on a salad drizzled with olive oil and balsamic vinegar. These Balsamic Beets side dish that will be everyone's favorite.

Serves 4

4 medium beets, peeled and halved

1 cup beef stock

1 sprig fresh thyme

1 teaspoon balsamic vinegar

1 teaspoon kosher salt

1 garlic clove, minced

½ teaspoon freshly ground black pepper

1   Place all of the ingredients into the pressure cooker; secure the lid.

2   When pressure is achieved, set a timer for 10 minutes.

3   When the cook time is complete and pressure is fully released, remove the lid with caution.

4   Remove and discard the thyme and serve hot or cold.

Artichokes in Lemon

Dip these artichokes in garlic butter and splash with lemon. Serve as a starter to any meal or as a light lunch.

Serves 3 to 6

3 whole artichokes

½ cup white wine

½ cup chicken stock

Fresh juice and zest from 1 lemon

1 sprig fresh thyme

3 whole black peppercorns

1   Wash the artichokes under cold water.

2   Using a sharp knife, cut the stems off close to the base.

3   Cut off the top inch of the artichoke and trim the thorny tips of the petals.

4   Add the wine, stock, lemon juice, and lemon zest to the pressure cooker.

5   Place the artichokes into the pressure cooker, stem side down.

6   Add the thyme and peppercorns to the pressure cooker; secure the lid.

7   When pressure is achieved, set a timer for 20 minutes.

8   When the cook time is complete and pressure is fully released, remove the lid with caution.

9   Remove and discard the thyme.

10   Serve hot, with drawn butter or mayonnaise, or cold.

Corn Pudding

Corn Pudding is delicious next to a ham or baked chicken. A real home-style side dish just like your Grandma made, it can be jazzed up with pan-seared scallops.

Serves 4

1 cup water

3 tablespoons unsalted butter, melted

4 ounces cream cheese, softened

One 8.5-ounce box corn muffin mix

One 8.5-ounce can creamed corn

¾ cup sour cream

2 cups frozen corn

1 teaspoon kosher salt

½ teaspoon freshly ground black pepper

1   Pour the water into the pressure cooker.

2   Apply nonstick cooking spray to a 3-quart stainless steel bowl.

3   Place the unsalted butter, cream cheese, corn muffin mix, creamed corn, sour cream, frozen corn, kosher salt, and pepper into the bowl; mix well.

4   Cover the bowl with aluminum foil.

5   Place the bowl into the pressure cooker; secure the lid.

6   When pressure is achieved, set a timer for 15 minutes.

7   When the cook time is complete and pressure is fully released, remove the lid with caution.

8   Serve immediately.

Sweet and Savory Carrots

We love these carrots next to pork loins and hearty beef dishes. Sweet and tender carrots in a sweet and savory sauce.

Serves 4 to 6

2½ pounds carrots, peeled and cut diagonally into 1-inch pieces

½ cup chicken stock

½ teaspoon kosher salt

½ teaspoon soy sauce

½ teaspoon freshly ground black pepper

1 tablespoon brown sugar

1 tablespoon unsalted butter

1   Place all of the ingredients into the pressure cooker; secure the lid.

2   When pressure is achieved, set a timer for 5 minutes.

3   When the cook time is complete and pressure is fully released, remove the lid with caution.

4   Serve immediately.

Lemon Dill Green Beans

Kids and adults alike won't be able to resist these green beans, with a fresh and lively taste from the lemon. They go wonderfully with baked chicken or salmon.

Serves 4 to 6

2 pounds green beans, trimmed

¼ cup chicken stock

¼ cup fresh lemon juice

1 teaspoon lemon zest

2 garlic cloves, minced

½ teaspoon kosher salt

½ teaspoon freshly ground black pepper

1 tablespoon extra-virgin olive oil

1 teaspoon chopped fresh dill

1   Place all of the ingredients into the pressure cooker; secure the lid.

2   When pressure is achieved, set a timer for 5 minutes.

3   When the cook time is complete and pressure is fully released, remove the lid with caution.

4   Serve immediately.

Creamed Corn with Pesto

The pesto gives this classic pizzazz. This dish pairs nicely with all your holiday favorites, from Thanksgiving turkey to Easter ham.

Serves 4 to 6

8 ears corn

1 cup chicken stock

1 teaspoon kosher salt

½ teaspoon freshly ground black pepper

1 teaspoon sugar

1 small onion, diced

1 tablespoon unsalted butter

2 ounces cream cheese

1 tablespoon fresh pesto

1   Using a knife, remove the corn from the cobs.

2   Place corn kernels, corncobs, stock, kosher salt, pepper, sugar, and onion into the pressure cooker; secure the lid.

3   When pressure is achieved, set a timer for 10 minutes.

4   When the cook time is complete and pressure is fully released, remove the lid with caution.

5   Add the unsalted butter and cream cheese to the pressure cooker; secure the lid.

6   When pressure is achieved, set a timer for 3 minutes.

7   When the cook time is complete and pressure is fully released, remove the lid with caution.

8   Using tongs, remove the corncobs and discard them.

9   Using an immersion blender, purée the corn until it reaches the desired consistency, stir in the pesto.

10   Serve immediately.

Hummus

For the ultimate party snack, arrange pita, sliced red bell peppers, carrots, and cucumbers with hummus for dipping. This recipe also works great as a spread on a veggie wrap.

Serves 6 to 8

1 cup dried garbanzo beans

1 teaspoon baking soda

Fresh juice and zest from 1 lemon

2 garlic cloves, minced

1 teaspoon ground cumin

3 teaspoons kosher salt

½ teaspoon cayenne pepper

5 cups water

2 tablespoons tahini paste

1 cup extra-virgin olive oil

1 In a medium bowl, cover the garbanzo beans with water and baking soda; let soak for an hour.

2 Rinse the beans and transfer to the pressure cooker.

3 Add the lemon juice, lemon zest, garlic, cumin, kosher salt, cayenne, and water to the pressure cooker; secure the lid.

4 When pressure is achieved, set a timer for 30 minutes.

5 When the cook time is complete and pressure is fully released, remove the lid with caution.

6 Drain the beans and transfer them to a food processor fitted with a metal chopping blade. Add the tahini paste.

7 Process the beans, slowly drizzling in the olive oil to create an emulsion.

8 Transfer the hummus to a plate and serve.

Cuban Black Beans

Pair this with my Chicken and Yellow Rice (page 148) for a Mexicali dinner from your own kitchen. For a little heat, garnish with minced jalapeños and a dash of fresh lime juice.

Serves 4 to 6

1 pound dried black beans

5 cups beef stock

1 medium onion, diced

2 garlic cloves, minced

1 red bell pepper, diced

2 tablespoons chopped fresh cilantro

1 teaspoon kosher salt

½ teaspoon freshly ground black pepper

1 teaspoon ground cumin

One 14.5-ounce can petite diced tomatoes with olive oil

1   Place all of the ingredients into the pressure cooker; secure the lid.

2   When pressure is achieved, set a timer for 50 minutes.

3   When the cook time is complete and pressure is fully released, remove the lid with caution.

4   Serve immediately.

7 min.

Garlic Mashed Potatoes

You can't go wrong with these fluffy mashed potatoes, which pair with virtually everything from steak to chicken.

Serves 4 to 6

1 pound Yukon Gold potatoes, peeled and halved

½ cup chicken stock

2 garlic cloves

½ teaspoon kosher salt

½ teaspoon freshly ground black pepper

¼ cup heavy cream, heated

3 tablespoons unsalted butter

1 Place the potatoes, stock, garlic, kosher salt, and pepper into the pressure cooker; secure the lid.

2 When pressure is achieved, set a timer for 7 minutes.

3 When the cook time is complete and pressure is fully released, remove the lid with caution.

4 Drain the potatoes, add the cream and unsalted butter, and mash until the potatoes reach a smooth consistency.

5 Serve immediately.

Mashed Potatoes with Rutabaga

Another way to sneak in the veggies.
You already love mashed potatoes,
so why not add some extra nutrition?

Serves 4 to 6

6 Yukon Gold potatoes, peeled and halved

½ cup rutabaga, peeled and diced into 1-inch cubes

1 cup chicken stock

1 teaspoon kosher salt

½ teaspoon freshly ground black pepper

2 tablespoons heavy cream

2 tablespoons unsalted butter

1   Place the potatoes, rutabaga, stock, kosher salt, and pepper into the pressure cooker; secure the lid.

2   When pressure is achieved, set a timer for 10 minutes.

3   When the cook time is complete and pressure is fully released, remove the lid with caution.

4   Drain the potatoes.

5   Add the cream and unsalted butter to the potatoes and mash using a potato masher.

6   Serve immediately.

Parsnip Purée with Shallots

The cream cheese in this recipe blends beautifully with the parsnips to make a creamy side.

Serves 4 to 6

2-pounds parsnips, peeled and cut into 2-inch pieces

1 shallot, minced

⅓ cup chicken stock

½ teaspoon salt

½ teaspoon freshly ground pepper

2-ounces cream cheese

1   Place the parsnips, shallot, stock, kosher salt, and pepper into the pressure cooker; secure the lid.

2   When pressure is achieved, set a timer for 7 minutes.

3   When the cook time is complete and pressure is fully released, remove the lid with caution.

4   Drain the parsnips, then place them into a food processor.

5   Add the cream cheese to the food processor and purée until smooth.

6   Serve immediately.

45 min.

Southern Collard Greens

Serve these tasty greens with Carolina BBQ Brisket (page 88) for a summertime hit with real Southern flavor! Add in as much heat as you can take.

Serves 4 to 6

1 pound smoked pork neck bones

2 cups chicken stock

1 medium onion, quartered

1 large bunch collard greens, stems removed

1 teaspoon kosher salt

½ teaspoon freshly ground black pepper

½ teaspoon garlic powder

1 teaspoon pepper vinegar

1 tablespoon Sriracha sauce

1   Place the pork bones, stock, and onion into the pressure cooker; secure the lid.

2   When pressure is achieved, set a timer for 30 minutes.

3   When the cook time is complete and pressure is fully released, remove the lid with caution.

4   Remove the meat to a cutting board, cut the meat from the bones, and return the meat to the pressure cooker; discard the bones.

5   Add the collard greens, kosher salt, pepper, garlic powder, vinegar, and Sriracha to the pressure cooker; secure the lid.

6   When pressure is achieved, set a timer for 15 minutes.

7   When the cook time is complete and pressure is fully released, remove the lid with caution.

8   Serve immediately.

Polish Purple Cabbage

The pressure cooker pumps tons of juicy flavor into this cabbage. Let it do the work for you, in half the time. Polish Purple Cabbage is a great side dish for grilled pork chops.

Serves 4 to 6

1 head purple cabbage, sliced

3 apples, cored and quartered

1 large onion, sliced

2 cups beef stock

1 teaspoon sugar

1 teaspoon kosher salt

½ teaspoon freshly ground black pepper

1 tablespoon balsamic vinegar

1 teaspoon caraway seeds

1   Place the cabbage, apples, onion, stock, sugar, kosher salt, pepper, and vinegar into the pressure cooker; secure the lid.

2   When pressure is achieved, set a timer for 20 minutes.

3   When the cook time is complete and pressure is fully released, remove the lid with caution.

4   Stir in the caraway seeds and serve.

Stuffed Onions

These turkey-stuffed onions make a great addition to a potluck-style dinner. Leave the turkey out for a yummy side dish.

Serves 4

4 large purple onions

1 tablespoon extra-virgin olive oil

½ pound ground turkey

½ teaspoon kosher salt

¼ teaspoon freshly ground black pepper

½ teaspoon fresh tarragon leaves

8 large mushrooms, chopped fine

½ cup white wine

1 cup chicken stock, divided

1 teaspoon white balsamic vinegar

1   Cut the tops and bottoms off the onions, then peel off the two outer layers of each one.

2   Scoop out the center of each onion until 1 inch is left in the bottom.

3   Preheat the olive oil in the pressure cooker with the lid off.

4   Add the turkey to the pressure cooker and brown for 4 minutes, breaking up the meat with a wooden spoon; season with kosher salt, pepper, and tarragon while browning.

5   Add the mushrooms and begin to brown. Add the wine and ½ cup of the stock to the pan; cook for 6 minutes.

6   Stuff each onion with the mixture, then place the stuffed onions into the pressure cooker.

7   Add the remaining ½ cup stock and the vinegar to the pressure cooker; secure the lid.

8   When pressure is achieved, set a timer for 12 minutes.

9   When the cook time is complete and pressure is fully released, remove the lid with caution.

10 Serve the onions topped with some remaining stock.

Sesame Green Beans

These delicious gems pair wonderfully with our
Teriyaki Chicken and Rice (page 155). Change
up your everyday routine and enjoy the flavors.

Serves 4

1 pound green beans, trimmed

½ cup chicken stock

½ teaspoon kosher salt

½ teaspoon freshly ground
black pepper

Pinch of crushed red pepper
flakes

2 teaspoons rice wine vinegar

1 teaspoon sesame oil

1 teaspoon sesame seeds

1   Place the green beans, stock, kosher salt, pepper,
    red pepper flakes, vinegar, and sesame oil into the
    pressure cooker; secure the lid.

2   When pressure is achieved, set a timer for 3 minutes.

3   Meanwhile, toast the sesame seeds in a nonstick
    skillet until golden brown.

4   When the cook time is complete and pressure is fully
    released, remove the lid with caution.

5   Transfer the beans to a platter, sprinkle with the
    toasted sesame seeds, and serve.

Sweet Beets

Serve these beets hot as a side dish,
or chill to make the best salad topping!

Serves 4 to 6

1 pound beets, golden and/or red,
peeled and quartered

½ cup Rich Chicken Stock
(see page 41)

½ teaspoon kosher salt

½ teaspoon freshly ground
black pepper

1 teaspoon lemon zest

1 sprig fresh thyme

2 tablespoons unsalted butter

1   Place all of the ingredients into the pressure cooker;
secure the lid.

2   When pressure is achieved, set a timer for 10 minutes.

3   When the cook time is complete and pressure is fully
released, remove the lid with caution.

4   Remove and discard the thyme and serve.

Sweet Potato Casserole

Sweet potato casserole is a family favorite for all holiday get-togethers. This side doubles as a dessert! With this recipe, there's no need to buy the canned sweet potatoes.

Serves 4 to 6

4 sweet potatoes, peeled and quartered

1 cup chicken stock

½ cup orange juice

1 teaspoon kosher salt

½ teaspoon freshly ground black pepper

½ teaspoon ground cinnamon

2 tablespoons unsalted butter

2 cups mini marshmallows

1 Place the sweet potatoes, stock, orange juice, kosher salt, pepper, and cinnamon into the pressure cooker; secure the lid.

2 When pressure is achieved, set a timer for 10 minutes.

3 When the cook time is complete and pressure is fully released, remove the lid with caution.

4 Drain the sweet potatoes, add the unsalted butter, and mash the sweet potatoes using a potato masher.

5 Set oven to broil.

6 Apply nonstick cooking spray to an oven-safe casserole dish and place the mashed sweet potatoes into the casserole; top with marshmallows.

7 Place the casserole on the center rack of the oven and cook for 2 minutes, or until the marshmallows are lightly toasted.

8 Remove the casserole from the oven and serve.

Szechuan Veggies

These veggies are to die for when tossed with rice noodles or pasta. Great for a super-quick, healthy dinner.

Serves 4 to 6

3 cups broccoli florets

3 cups cauliflower florets

1 cup peeled and sliced carrots

1 red bell pepper, julienned

1 medium onion, thinly sliced

1 tablespoon sesame oil

1 tablespoon water

3 tablespoons oyster sauce

1 teaspoon soy sauce

1 tablespoon fresh ginger, grated

2 garlic cloves, minced

1 teaspoon crushed red pepper flakes

1   Place all ingredients into the pressure cooker, tossing well; secure the lid.

2   When pressure is achieved, set a timer for 3 minutes.

3   When the cook time is complete and pressure is fully released, remove the lid with caution.

4   Serve immediately.

Spaghetti Squash

This spaghetti squash holds its own as a side to a spicy chicken dish. A great substitute for pasta, it tastes so good you won't miss the carbs.

Serves 4

2 tablespoons unsalted butter, divided

1 large spaghetti squash, cut in half horizontally and seeds removed

¼ teaspoon kosher salt

¼ teaspoon freshly ground black pepper

2 cups water

1   Place 1 teaspoon of the butter on each half of squash.

2   Sprinkle both halves with kosher salt and pepper.

3   Pour the water into the pressure cooker.

4   Fit the pressure cooker with a stainless steel rack and place the squash on the rack, cut side up; secure the lid.

5   When pressure is achieved, set a timer for 10 minutes.

6   When the cook time is complete and pressure is fully released, remove the lid with caution.

7   Serve immediately.

Beet Greens

This side gets creative with the tops of beets.
Use the roots for our Sweet Beets recipe (page 191)!
Top off with a touch of pepper vinegar.

Serves 4 to 6

3 pounds beet tops, chopped into
2-inch pieces

1 smoked turkey wing, meat
chopped into ½-inch chunks

1 small sweet onion, chopped

½ cup chicken stock

½ teaspoon kosher salt

½ teaspoon cayenne pepper

Pinch of sugar

1   Place all of the ingredients, including the turkey wing
    bone, into the pressure cooker; stir, then secure the lid.

2   When pressure is achieved, set a timer for 10 minutes.

3   When the cook time is complete and pressure is fully
    released, remove the lid with caution.

4   Remove and discard the bone, and serve.

Tuscan Onions

Tuscan Onions are delicious next to my
Mediterranean Chicken with Orzo (page 62)!
As the perfect accent for any meal, your
family will ask for this dish again and again.

Serves 4

4 medium sweet onions, peeled

2 cups chicken stock

2 teaspoons balsamic vinegar

1 teaspoon kosher salt

½ teaspoon freshly ground
black pepper

2 sprigs fresh thyme

1 Cut off the top and bottom of each onion.

2 Place the onions, stock, vinegar, kosher salt, pepper,
and thyme into the pressure cooker; secure the lid.

3 When pressure is achieved, set a timer for 10 minutes.

4 When the cook time is complete and pressure is fully
released, remove the lid with caution.

5 Remove and discard the thyme and serve
immediately.

Italian Green Beans

Italian Green Beans pair nicely with my Chicken Cacciatore (page 56) and Garlic Mashed Potatoes (page 183) and are ready in a snap.

Serves 4

1 pound green beans, trimmed and cut into 1-inch pieces

1 teaspoon kosher salt

½ teaspoon freshly ground black pepper

1 small onion, diced

1 garlic clove, minced

1 pint cherry tomatoes, sliced

1 teaspoon lemon juice

½ cup chicken stock

½ teaspoon Italian seasoning

½ teaspoon red pepper flakes

1 Place all of the ingredients into the pressure cooker; secure the lid.

2 When pressure is achieved, set a timer for 3 minutes.

3 When the cook time is complete and pressure is fully released, remove the lid with caution.

4 Serve hot.

Warm Potato Salad

A more sophisticated approach to cold deli-style potato salad. This warm potato salad can be served next to the finest entrées.

Serves 4

1 pound fingerling potatoes

3 garlic cloves, sliced

2 teaspoons kosher salt

1 cup water

¼ cup peanut oil

1 cup champagne vinegar

1 tablespoon chopped fresh thyme leaves

1 small sweet onion, cut into ¼-inch chunks

3 tablespoons sugar

½ teaspoon freshly ground black pepper

1 small green onion, finely chopped

1   Place the potatoes, garlic, kosher salt, and water into the pressure cooker; secure the lid.

2   When pressure is achieved, set a timer for 3 minutes.

3   While the potatoes are cooking, combine the peanut oil, vinegar, thyme, onion, sugar, and pepper in a bowl; stir.

4   When the cook time is complete and pressure is fully released, remove the lid with caution.

5   Drain the potatoes. When cool enough to handle, slice them into ½-inch rounds and toss with the marinade.

6   Garnish with the green onion and serve warm.

Wild Rice Stuffing

Wild Rice Stuffing is a perfect side dish
to complement roast turkey or chicken.
It is easy enough to have most any night.

Serves 4 to 6

1 pound ground turkey

1 small onion, minced

1 celery stalk, chopped

1 teaspoon kosher salt

½ teaspoon freshly ground
black pepper

1 teaspoon poultry seasoning

1 cup dry wild rice, rinsed

3½ cups chicken stock

½ cup dried cranberries

½ cup pecans, chopped

2 fresh sage leaves, chopped

1 Add the turkey to the pressure cooker; cook for
3 minutes with the lid off, breaking up the turkey using
a wooden spoon.

2 Add the onion, celery, kosher salt, and pepper to the
pressure cooker; cook for an additional 2 minutes
while continuing to break up the turkey.

3 Add the poultry seasoning, rice, stock, cranberries,
pecans, and sage leaves to the pressure cooker;
secure the lid.

4 When pressure is achieved, set a timer for 30 minutes.

5 When the cook time is complete and pressure is fully
released, remove the lid with caution.

6 Stir and serve.

Southwestern Corn on the Cob

This side is perfect next to my Turkey Tacos (page 67) or Chipotle Chicken Burritos (page 76). Or, try cutting the corn off the cob and sprinkling the kernels on top of a Southwestern salad.

Serves 4 to 6

6 ears corn, husked

½ cup water

1 teaspoon kosher salt

½ teaspoon sugar

3 tablespoon unsalted butter

¼ teaspoon cayenne pepper

1 teaspoon fresh lime juice

½ teaspoon fresh cilantro

1   Place the corn, water, kosher salt, sugar, unsalted butter, and cayenne into the pressure cooker; secure the lid.

2   When pressure is achieved, set a timer for 6 minutes.

3   When the cook time is complete and pressure is fully released, remove the lid with caution.

4   Remove the corn to a platter, sprinkle with the lime juice and cilantro, and serve.

Black-Eyed Peas

A Southern favorite, these black-eyed peas are great with ham and greens. Top with chopped green onions and a dash of hot sauce.

Serves 6 to 8

1 pound dried black-eyed peas

5 cups chicken stock

4 ounces smoked pork neck bones

1 medium onion, diced

1 tablespoon red wine vinegar

3 garlic cloves, minced

1 teaspoon kosher salt

½ teaspoon freshly ground black pepper

1 teaspoon crushed red pepper flakes

1 sprig fresh thyme

1   Place all of the ingredients into the pressure cooker; secure the lid

2   When pressure is achieved, set a timer for 20 minutes.

3   When the cook time is complete and pressure is fully released, remove the lid with caution.

4   Remove and discard the thyme and serve immediately.

Brussels Sprouts with Onions

Delicious next to salmon or chicken, these Brussels sprouts add a fun texture to your plate. Serve this dish with a side of horseradish sauce.

Serves 4

1½ pounds Brussels sprouts, trimmed

One 10-ounce bag frozen pearl onions

1 cup beef stock

1 teaspoon freshly ground black pepper

1 sprig fresh thyme

1   Place all of the ingredients into the pressure cooker; secure the lid.

2   When pressure is achieved, set a timer for 5 minutes.

3   When the cook time is complete and pressure is fully released, remove the lid with caution.

4   Remove and discard the thyme and serve.

Grains and Pasta

Couscous with Cauliflower and Chickpeas

This classic Middle Eastern side dish is fabulous with chicken and lamb, or just as a vegetarian meal on its own.

Serves 6

1 cup Israeli (pearl) couscous

1 large onion, chopped

1 teaspoon kosher salt

½ teaspoon freshly ground black pepper

5 teaspoons curry powder

Two 15.5-ounce cans garbanzo beans, drained

Two 10-ounce cans tomatoes with green chilis

One 13.5-ounce can light coconut milk

3 cups chicken or vegetable stock

6 cups cauliflower florets

½ cup chopped fresh cilantro

1   Place the couscous, onion, kosher salt, pepper, curry powder, garbanzo beans, tomatoes with green chilis, coconut milk, and stock into the pressure cooker; secure the lid.

2   When pressure is achieved, set a timer for 4 minutes.

3   When the cook time is complete and pressure is fully released, open the lid with caution.

4   Stir in the cauliflower and secure the lid again. Let sit in the hot pressure cooker for 3 minutes.

5   Sprinkle with the cilantro and serve hot.

Broccoli Risotto

Broccoli Risotto is the perfect side dish for your favorite roast, or a light lunch to take to work.

Serves 4

2 tablespoons extra-virgin olive oil

1 small onion, chopped

1 cup dry Arborio rice

1 teaspoon kosher salt

1 cup chicken stock

1 cup whole milk

1 cup grated Cheddar cheese

¾ cup broccoli florets

1   Place the olive oil, onion, rice, kosher salt, stock, and milk into the pressure cooker; secure the lid.

2   When pressure is achieved, set a timer for 8 minutes.

3   When the cook time is complete and pressure is fully released, remove the lid with caution.

4   Add the cheese and stir well.

5   Add the broccoli to the pressure cooker; secure the lid.

6   When pressure is achieved, set a timer for 3 minutes.

7   When the cook time is complete and pressure is fully released, remove the lid with caution.

8   Serve immediately.

21 min.

Brown Rice Pilaf with Lentils

A hearty and delicious side, Brown Rice Pilaf with Lentils is versatile for any meal. For those who thought cooking brown rice was difficult.

Serves 4 to 6

1 cup dry brown basmati rice

2 cups water

1 teaspoon kosher salt

1 tablespoon extra-virgin olive oil

1 cup dried lentils

2 garlic cloves, minced

2 carrots, peeled and diced

1 medium onion, diced

1 cup freshly diced tomatoes

2 cups vegetable stock

¼ teaspoon dried thyme

2 celery stalks, diced

1 tablespoon chopped fresh parsley

1   Place the rice, water, kosher salt, and olive oil into the pressure cooker; secure the lid.

2   When pressure is achieved, set a timer for 15 minutes.

3   When the cook time is complete and pressure is fully released, remove the lid with caution.

4   Add the lentils, garlic, carrots, onion, tomatoes, stock, thyme, and celery to the pressure cooker; secure the lid.

5   When pressure is achieved, set a timer for 6 minutes.

6   When the cook time is complete and pressure is fully released, remove the lid with caution.

7   Stir well, top with the parsley, and serve.

Cheesy Grits

This Southern staple can be served for breakfast, lunch, or dinner—alongside eggs and pancakes or fried chicken and shrimp. This catchall is warm, filling, and a reminder of home.

Serves 2 to 4

2½ cups water

1 cup stone-ground grits

2 tablespoons unsalted butter

2 tablespoons half-and-half

1 cup grated Parmesan cheese

¼ teaspoon kosher salt

¼ teaspoon freshly ground black pepper

1   Place about ½ cup water into the pressure cooker; set a 3-quart metal bowl inside the pressure cooker.

2   Add the 2½ cups water to the bowl, along with the grits, unsalted butter, and half-and-half; secure the pressure cooker lid.

3   When pressure is achieved, set a timer for 15 minutes.

4   When the cook time is complete and pressure is fully released, remove the lid with caution.

5   Carefully remove the bowl from the pressure cooker and stir in cheese, kosher salt, and pepper.

6   Serve immediately.

Spicy Bulgur Pilaf

Bulgur is a healthy and delicious substitute for rice. A great side dish to serve with a vegetable stir-fry.

Serves 4 to 6

1 medium onion, chopped

1 garlic clove, sliced

1 cup dry bulgur

½ teaspoon turmeric powder

½ teaspoon cumin seeds

1½ cups chicken stock

1 tablespoon lemon zest

½ cup black olives, pitted and sliced

¼ cup fresh lemon juice

1 tablespoon chopped fresh cilantro leaves

1 Place the onion, garlic, bulgur, turmeric, cumin, stock, lemon zest, olives, and lemon juice into the pressure cooker; secure the lid.

2 When pressure is achieved, set a timer for 6 minutes.

3 When the cook time is complete and pressure is fully released, remove the lid with caution.

4 Fluff the pilaf using a fork, top with the cilantro, and serve.

Garlic Mushroom Quinoa

12 min.

Quinoa is the perfect protein, packed with amino acids. It brings the needed nutrition for active vegetarians.

Serves 4 to 6

1 tablespoon extra-virgin olive oil

1 pound baby Portobello mushrooms, thinly sliced

5 garlic cloves, minced

1 cup dry quinoa, rinsed

2 cups chicken, beef, or vegetable stock

¼ teaspoon kosher salt

¼ teaspoon freshly ground black pepper

½ teaspoon dried thyme

¼ teaspoons red pepper flakes

2 tablespoons grated Parmesan cheese

1   Preheat olive oil in the pressure cooker with the lid off, add the mushrooms and garlic; and sauté for 5 minutes.

2   Add the quinoa, stock, kosher salt, pepper, and thyme to the pressure cooker; secure the lid.

3   When pressure is achieved, set a timer for 12 minutes.

4   When the cook time is complete and pressure is fully released, remove the lid with caution.

5   Stir in cheese and pepper flakes.

6   Serve immediately.

Perfect Brown Rice

Brown Rice is a super food! Rich with many vitamins and minerals, this recipe is an excellent source of manganese, and selenium. It comes out perfectly every time.

Serves 7

3 cups dry brown rice, rinsed and drained

6 cups water

1 teaspoon kosher salt

1 tablespoon extra-virgin olive oil

1   Place all of the ingredients into the pressure cooker; secure the lid.

2   When pressure is achieved, set a timer for 20 minutes.

3   When the cook time is complete and pressure is fully released, remove the lid with caution.

4   Serve immediately.

Wheat Berry Salad

This mighty fiber salad will satisfy and satiate.
Prepare ahead for a quick and easy side dish.
Top with blue cheese or a crumbly feta.

Serves 4 to 6

1 cup dry wheat berries, rinsed

2 cups water

½ teaspoon kosher salt

1 small onion, chopped

1 English cucumber, seeded
and chopped

1 medium tomato, diced

½ teaspoon chopped fresh mint
leaves

1 teaspoon fresh lemon juice

½ teaspoon garlic kosher salt

½ teaspoon freshly ground
black pepper

2 tablespoons extra-virgin olive oil

1 Place the wheat berries, water, and kosher salt into
the pressure cooker; secure the lid.

2 When pressure is achieved, set a timer for 35 minutes.

3 When the cook time is complete and pressure is
fully released, remove the lid with caution.

4 Transfer the wheat berries to a large bowl; let cool
to room temperature.

5 Add the onion, cucumber, tomato, mint, lemon juice,
garlic kosher salt, pepper, and olive oil to the bowl;
toss well.

6 Chill for 30 minutes before serving.

20 min.

Wild Rice with Mushrooms

Who knew this nutrient-rich grass, which we call rice, would be so delicious and easy to prepare with a pressure cooker? Get creative at your farmers market and bring home several different kinds of mushrooms to use.

Serves 4 to 6

2 cups dry wild rice

4 cups beef stock

1 cup mushrooms, sliced

1 small onion, diced

2 tablespoons unsalted butter

½ cup slivered almonds

2 tablespoons chopped green onion

1   Place the rice, stock, mushrooms, and onion into the pressure cooker; secure the lid.

2   When pressure is achieved, set a timer for 20 minutes.

3   When the cook time is complete and pressure is fully released, remove the lid with caution.

4   Add the unsalted butter and almonds and stir.

5   Garnish with the green onions and serve.

Quinoa with Kale and Squash

Super foods assemble! Eat your way to nutrition; in a pressure cooker, even more of the nutrients are locked in.

Serves 6 to 8

1 pound butternut squash, peeled, diced, and seeded

3 cups stemmed, chopped kale

¼ cup fresh lime juice

1 garlic clove, minced

¼ teaspoon sea kosher salt

½ cup dry quinoa, rinsed

¼ cup dried cranberries

1 cup vegetable stock

1   Place all of the ingredients into the pressure cooker; secure the lid.

2   When pressure is achieved, set a timer for 10 minutes.

3   When the cook time is complete and pressure is fully released, remove the lid with caution.

4   Serve immediately.

Farro Pilaf

This ancient grain will bring your diet to new levels of nutrition and deliciousness. Farro Pilaf is great for those who want more from their side dish than just flavor.

Serves 4 to 6

1 tablespoon extra-virgin olive oil

1 small onion, sliced

1 cup mushrooms, sliced

2 garlic cloves, minced

1 cup dry farro

2 cups vegetable stock

¼ teaspoon sea kosher salt

¼ teaspoon freshly ground black pepper

1 Preheat the olive oil in the pressure cooker. Add the onion, mushrooms, and garlic.

2 Sauté for 5 minutes, add the farro, and cook for an additional minute.

3 Add the stock, kosher salt, and pepper to the pressure cooker; secure the lid.

4 When pressure is achieved, set a timer for 12 minutes.

5 When the cook time is complete and pressure is fully released, remove the lid with caution.

6 Serve immediately.

6 min.

Perfect White Rice

One of my favorite features of the pressure cooker is the rice function. Rice is cooked to perfection—fluffy and delicious. Add a side of chicken and teriyaki sauce for a quick Asian flair.

Serves 4

2 cups dry long-grain rice, rinsed

2 cups water

Pinch of kosher salt

1 teaspoon extra-virgin olive oil

1   Add the rice, water, kosher salt, and olive oil to the pressure cooker; secure the lid.

2   When pressure is achieved, set a timer for 6 minutes.

3   When the cook time is complete and pressure is fully released, remove the lid with caution.

4   Fluff rice and serve at once.

Mushroom Farro Risotto

This cheesy medley will melt in your mouth. The mushrooms bring protein and the onion brings flavor.

Serves 4 to 6

1 tablespoon extra-virgin olive oil, divided

10 ounces fresh mushrooms, sliced

1 medium sweet onion, thinly sliced

2 cloves garlic, minced

½ teaspoon kosher salt

1 cup dry farro, rinsed

1 cup dry white wine

1 ½ cups chicken stock

⅓ cup grated Parmesan cheese

1 tablespoons unsalted butter

1 Preheat the pressure cooker with the oil, then add the mushrooms and onion, and cook for 4 minutes.

2 Add the garlic and kosher salt and cook for 2 minutes longer.

3 Add the farro, wine, and stock to the pressure cooker; secure the lid.

4 When pressure is achieved, set a timer for 10 minutes.

5 When the cook time is complete and pressure is fully released, remove the lid with caution.

6 Add the cheese and unsalted butter and stir until melted.

7 Serve immediately.

Southwestern Brown Rice Salad

Southwestern Brown Rice Salad is great as a warm side or served cold, drizzled with a creamy chipotle ranch.

Serves 6

RICE

1 cup dry brown rice, rinsed

2 cups chicken stock

2 ears corn, husked

1 teaspoon kosher salt

½ teaspoon freshly ground black pepper

1 teaspoon ground cumin

2 garlic cloves, minced

SALAD

2 (15-ounce) cans black beans, rinsed and drained

1 red bell pepper, finely chopped

5 green onions, thinly sliced

1 small jalapeño, seeds and membranes removed, minced

DRESSING

Fresh juice of one lime

3 tablespoons extra-virgin olive oil

½ teaspoon garlic kosher salt

3 tablespoons chopped fresh cilantro

FOR THE RICE:

1 Place all of the ingredients in the pressure cooker; secure the lid.

2 When pressure is achieved, set a timer for 20 minutes.

FOR THE SALAD:

1 In a large bowl, combine all of the ingredients.

FOR THE DRESSING:

1 In a small bowl, combine all of the ingredients.

TO FINISH:

1 When the cook time is complete and pressure is fully released, remove the lid with caution.

2 Remove the ears of corn and place them in a bowl of cold water.

3 Fluff the rice and let it cool for at least 10 minutes.

4 With a sharp knife, remove the corn from the cobs and add to the salad.

5 Add the rice to the salad, then toss with the dressing.

6 Serve warm or cold.

Asparagus Risotto

Do you see a trend here? I like to switch up the veggies in our risotto. Feel free to play with your favorites to make your own creations.

Serves 4

1 tablespoon unsalted butter

2 cups dry Arborio rice, rinsed

1 shallot, minced

8 ounces thin asparagus, cut into 1-inch pieces

½ teaspoon sea kosher salt

½ teaspoon freshly ground black pepper

2 cups chicken stock

¼ cup grated Parmesan cheese

1   Place the butter in the pressure cooker and melt.

2   Add the rice and the shallot to the butter and cook for 2 minutes.

3   Add the asparagus, kosher salt, pepper, and stock to the pressure cooker; secure the lid.

4   When pressure is achieved, set a timer for 8 minutes.

5   When cook time is complete and pressure is fully released, remove the lid with caution.

6   Stir in the cheese and serve hot.

Quinoa Tabbouleh

This light, fresh-tasting Arabian vegetarian salad will perk up your palate. It's the perfect choice for that sweltering summer day when it's too hot to cook.

Serves 4

½ cup dry quinoa, rinsed

1 cup vegetable stock

2 cups diced unpeeled English cucumber

½ cup thinly sliced celery

½ cup finely chopped red onion

¼ cup chopped fresh mint

¼ cup chopped fresh parsley

¼ cup pine nuts, toasted

2 tablespoons extra-virgin olive oil

1 teaspoon lemon zest

2 tablespoons fresh lemon juice

¼ teaspoon kosher salt

¼ teaspoon crushed red pepper flakes

½ cup unsalted canned chickpeas, drained

4 ounces feta cheese, crumbled

Lemon wedges (optional) for serving

1 Preheat the pressure cooker, add the quinoa, and toast for several minutes.

2 Pour the stock into the pressure cooker; secure the lid.

3 When pressure is achieved, set a timer for 5 minutes.

4 While the quinoa is cooking, toss the cucumber, celery, red onion, mint, parsley, pine nuts, olive oil, lemon zest, lemon juice, kosher salt, red pepper flakes, and chickpeas in a large bowl.

5 When the cook time is complete and pressure is fully released, remove the lid with caution.

6 Let the quinoa cool for 10 minutes, and then toss with the vegetables.

7 Sprinkle the tabbouleh with the feta and serve with the lemon wedges.

Red Quinoa Citrus Salad

This zesty salad is super filling because of the quinoa. The cool freshness will tingle your taste buds.

Serves 4

1 cup dry red quinoa, rinsed

2 cups vegetable stock

Fresh zest and juice from 3 limes

½ teaspoon sugar

1 jalapeño, seeds and membrane removed, minced

2 garlic cloves, minced

¼ teaspoon ground cumin

1 teaspoon kosher salt

⅔ cup extra-virgin olive oil

1 bunch cilantro, stemmed and finely chopped

½ cup citrus segments, such as from mandarin oranges, navel oranges, and grapefruit

1 small red onion, minced

1 Place the quinoa, stock, and lime zest into the pressure cooker; secure the lid.

2 When pressure is achieved, set a timer for 7 minutes.

3 Meanwhile, in a small bowl, whisk together the lime juice, sugar, jalapeño, garlic, cumin, and kosher salt.

4 While continuing to whisk, slowly drizzle in the olive oil in to make a vinaigrette.

5 When the cook time is complete and pressure is fully released, remove the lid with caution.

6 Fluff the quinoa and let cool for 10 minutes.

7 Toss the quinoa with the cilantro, citrus segments, and red onion.

8 Toss well with vinaigrette.

9 Serve warm or cold.

Pearl Barley Vegetable Medley

Serve this vegetable dish hot or cold.
This hearty side is not only delicious but also
loaded with vitamins, minerals, and protein.

Serves 4

½ cup pearl barley, rinsed

2 cups beef or vegetable stock

1 cup corn kernels

1 small onion, diced

1 green bell pepper, diced

1 carrot, peeled and shredded

1 tomato, seeded and diced

1 tablespoon chopped fresh
parsley

¼ teaspoon kosher salt

¼ teaspoon dried thyme

1   Place all of the ingredients into the pressure cooker;
    secure the lid.

2   When pressure is achieved, set a timer for 18 minutes.

3   When the cook time is complete and pressure is fully
    released, remove the lid with caution.

4   Serve hot or cold.

Greek-Style Farro Salad

Put a new twist on Greek salad by adding farro to the mix. This nutty grain will complement any entrée, but it's also great alone sprinkled with feta as a meal in itself.

Serves 4 to 6

1 cup dry farro

2 cups vegetable stock

2 tablespoons extra-virgin olive oil

2 garlic cloves, minced

1 teaspoon white wine vinegar or lemon juice

¼ teaspoon dried oregano

¼ teaspoon kosher salt

¼ teaspoon freshly ground black pepper

1 pint heirloom grape tomatoes

1 small red onion, chopped

1 cucumber, peeled, seeded and chopped

4 pepperoncini, chopped

½ cup pitted kalamata olives, chopped

1 Place the farro and stock into the pressure cooker; secure the lid.

2 When pressure is achieved, set a timer for 12 minutes.

3 Meanwhile, in a small bowl, combine the olive oil, garlic, vinegar, oregano, kosher salt, and pepper; mix well.

4 When the cook time is complete and pressure is fully released, open the lid with caution.

5 Let the farro cool for 10 minutes , then fluff with a fork and add the tomatoes, red onion, cucumber, pepperoncini, and olives; toss with dressing and chill.

6 Serve when chilled.

Cilantro-Chili Jasmine Rice

This savory Southwestern rice dish is excellent to serve in burritos, or as a side to your favorite Mexican dish.

Serves 4

2 cups dry jasmine rice, rinsed

2 cups chicken stock

1 jalapeño, seeded and minced

1 garlic clove, minced

4 green onions, sliced

Zest from 1 lime

½ teaspoon kosher salt

1 bunch cilantro, stemmed and finely chopped

1   Place the rice, stock, jalapeño, garlic, green onions, lime zest, and kosher salt into the pressure cooker; secure the lid.

2   When pressure is achieved, set a timer for 8 minutes.

3   When the cook time is complete and pressure is fully released, open the lid with caution.

4   Toss the hot rice with fresh cilantro. Serve hot or cold.

Asian Black Rice Salad

When cooking traditional black rice, it's helpful to marinate the rice. With this method, the pressure cooker does the marinating for you, packing every grain with the flavors of the vegetable stock.

Serves 6

1 cup black rice, rinsed

2 cups vegetable stock

SALAD

1 cup shelled edamame

1 yellow bell pepper, seeded and diced

1 (15-ounce) can mandarin oranges, drained, liquid reserved

2 green onions, sliced

¼ cup chopped fresh cilantro

DRESSING

1½ tablespoons rice wine vinegar

1 tablespoon orange juice

¼ teaspoon soy sauce

1 teaspoon reserved mandarin juice

1 teaspoon freshly grated ginger

1 garlic clove, minced

1 teaspoon sesame oil

¼ cup extra-virgin olive oil

1 Place the rice and stock into the pressure cooker; secure the lid.

2 When pressure is achieved, set a timer for 20 minutes.

FOR THE SALAD:

1 Place all of the ingredients in a large bowl.

FOR THE DRESSING:

1 Add the vinegar, orange juice, soy sauce, reserved mandarin juice, ginger, garlic and sesame oil to the carafe of a blender.

2 Turn on the blender and process for 1 minute.

3 Slowly drizzle the olive oil through the feed tube.

4 When all of the oil has been added, continue blending for another 30 seconds.

5 When the cook time is complete and pressure is fully released, open the lid with caution.

6 Fluff the rice and let it cool for 20 minutes.

7 Add the rice to the salad mixture and then toss well with the dressing.

8 Serve immediately.

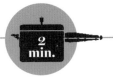

Maple Apple Steel-Cut Oats

These cinnamon-sweet steel-cut oats can be eaten as a side or alone for breakfast. The perfect way to start a cold winter day.

Serves 4

1 cup old-fashioned steel-cut oats

1½ cups water

1½ cups low-fat milk

Pinch of kosher salt

½ cup peeled and diced apples

1 tablespoon maple syrup

1 tablespoon unsalted butter

¼ teaspoon cinnamon

1 Place all of the ingredients into the pressure cooker; stir, then secure the lid.

2 When pressure is achieved, set a timer for 2 minutes.

3 When the cook time is complete and pressure is fully released, remove the lid with caution.

4 Stir and serve.

Four-Grain Mushroom Trifolati

Four-Grain Mushroom Trifolati is best made with my favorite mushroom, the hearty cremini, but any mushrooms will work. Be creative and find your favorite.

Serves 4

⅓ cup steel-cut oats

⅓ cup Arborio rice

⅓ cup farro

⅓ cup pearl barley

2 tablespoons extra-virgin olive oil

2 garlic cloves, minced

1 shallot, minced

10 ounces mushrooms, sliced

½ teaspoon kosher salt

¼ teaspoon freshly ground black pepper

½ cup dry white wine

2 cups beef stock

½ cup grated Parmesan cheese

½ cup chopped flat-leaf parsley

1 Rinse and drain the oats, rice, farro, and barley.

2 Preheat the pressure cooker, add the olive oil and grains, brown them for 2-3 minutes.

3 Add the garlic, shallot, and mushrooms and sauté, stirring, for several minutes.

4 Season the mushrooms with kosher salt and pepper.

5 Add the wine and deglaze, scraping up all the little bits from the bottom of the pan.

6 Add the stock to the pressure cooker; stir, then secure the lid.

7 When pressure is achieved, set a timer for 15 minutes.

8 When the cook time is complete and pressure is fully released, open the lid with caution.

9 Stir in the cheese and parsley and serve at once.

Lemony Wheat Berries with Brussels Sprouts

High in dietary fiber, protein, and iron, wheat berries are the filling component in this yummy side. Lemony Wheat Berries with Brussels Sprouts can be served hot or cold next to chicken or seasoned tofu.

Serves 4

1 cup dry red wheat berries, rinsed

2 cups vegetable or chicken stock

2 tablespoons extra-virgin olive oil

1 shallot, minced

1 pound Brussels sprouts, trimmed and quartered

1 tablespoon fresh lemon juice

½ teaspoon kosher salt

¼ teaspoon freshly ground black pepper

1   Place the wheat berries and stock into the pressure cooker; secure the lid.

2   When pressure has been achieved, set a timer for 30 minutes.

3   While the wheat berries are cooking, in a sauté pan, heat the olive oil over medium heat.

4   Add the shallot and Brussels sprouts and cook for several minutes, until starting to brown.

5   Season the Brussels sprouts with the lemon juice, kosher salt, and pepper. Set aside.

6   When the cook time is complete and pressure is fully released, open the lid with caution.

7   Stir the Brussels sprouts into the grain. Mix well.

8   Serve hot or cold.

Cilantro-Lime Quinoa Salad

Quinoa, the ancient grain, is a perfect food. It contains all twelve amino acids. Serve as a side or as a meal topped with grilled salmon.

Serves 4

1 cup dry quinoa, rinsed

1½ cups chicken stock

½ teaspoon ground cumin

Fresh zest and juice from 2 limes

½ teaspoon kosher salt

½ teaspoon freshly ground black pepper

½ cup extra-virgin olive oil

1 pint grape tomatoes, diced

One 15-ounce can black beans, rinsed and drained

1 jalapeño, seeded and minced

1 garlic clove, minced

5 green onions, thinly sliced

½ cup chopped fresh cilantro

1 ripe avocado, diced

1   Place the quinoa, stock, cumin, and lime zest into the pressure cooker; secure the lid.

2   When pressure is achieved, set a timer for 7 minutes.

3   While the quinoa is cooking, in a small bowl, add the lime juice, kosher salt, and pepper. Slowly whisk the olive oil into the juice.

4   In a large bowl, toss the tomatoes, beans, jalapeño, garlic, green onions, cilantro, and avocado.

5   When the cook time is complete and pressure is fully released, open the lid with caution.

6   Fluff the quinoa and let cool for 10 minutes.

7   Toss the quinoa with the tomato-bean mixture, then toss with the dressing.

8   Serve at once.

Desserts

Mixed Berry Cobbler

I like to mix berries in this recipe, combining sweet blueberries with tart raspberries, but you can switch up the mixture to your liking. The cobbler is even more delicious the next morning, served cold, next to a cup of tea.

Serves 8

One 12-ounce bag frozen mixed berries

¾ cup sugar

3 teaspoons quick-cooking tapioca

1 teaspoon orange zest

TOPPING

2 cups buttermilk biscuit mix

⅓ cup whole milk

3 tablespoons sugar

3 tablespoons unsalted butter, melted

1 teaspoon vanilla extract

1 Spray a 2-quart stainless steel bowl or baking insert with nonstick cooking spray.

2 Place the berries, sugar, tapioca, and orange zest in the bowl; mix well.

3 In a separate large bowl, combine all of the ingredients for the topping. Mix well and pour the topping over the berry mixture; cover the bowl with foil.

4 Pour about 2 cups of water into the pressure cooker, and carefully insert the bowl; secure the lid.

5 When pressure is achieved, set a timer for 25 minutes.

6 When the cook time is complete and pressure is fully released, remove the lid with caution.

7 Serve hot or cold.

Mocha Chip Cheesecake

This Mocha Chip Cheesecake isn't just for coffee lovers. The sweet chocolate complements the coffee in this creamy indulgence. Pair it with a cup of coffee or your favorite red wine.

Serves 4

1 cup crumbled chocolate wafer cookies

¼ cup unsalted butter, melted

⅓ cup sugar

3 tablespoons powdered sugar

Three 8-ounce packages cream cheese

3 large eggs

½ cup sour cream

1 tablespoon instant coffee granules

1 tablespoon cornstarch

1 cup mini chocolate chips

1   In a food processor, process the chocolate wafers and unsalted butter to a fine crumb.

2   Spray a 7-inch spring form pan with nonstick cooking spray.

3   Press the cookie mixture into the bottom of the pan.

4   Using a mixer, cream together the sugar, powdered sugar, and cream cheese together until smooth.

5   Mix in the eggs one at a time. Add the sour cream, coffee granules, and cornstarch; mix until smooth.

6   Stir in the chocolate chips, then pour the batter into the prepared pan.

7   Wrap the pan well with foil. Pour about 1 cup of water into the pressure cooker.

8   Add the pan to the pressure cooker; secure the lid.

9   When pressure is achieved, set a timer for 30 minutes.

10   When the cook time is complete and pressure is fully released, remove the lid with caution.

11   Using tongs, remove the pan from the pressure cooker. Chill for 3 hours before serving.

Chocolate Pots de Crème

This romantic dessert calls for orange zest, but if oranges are out of season, you can always substitute ½ teaspoon of pure orange extract.

Serves 4

2 ounces bittersweet chocolate, finely chopped

1 cup heavy cream

1 cup whole milk

4 large egg yolks

2 tablespoons sugar

½ teaspoon orange zest

⅛ teaspoon kosher salt

1   Apply nonstick cooking spray to four ½-cup ramekins; set aside.

2   Place the chocolate into a small, heat-resistant mixing bowl.

3   Pour the cream and milk into a saucepan over medium heat.

4   When the cream begins to simmer, pour it into the bowl with the chocolate; stir until smooth.

5   In a separate medium bowl, combine the egg yolks, sugar, orange zest, and kosher salt.

6   Slowly pour the chocolate mixture into the yolk mixture; mix well, then divide the mixture among the ramekins.

7   Wrap each ramekin in aluminum foil.

8   Pour about 1 cup of water into the pressure cooker and stack the ramekins inside the pressure cooker; secure the lid.

9   When pressure is achieved, set a timer for 10 minutes.

10   When the cook time is complete and pressure is fully released, remove the lid with caution.

11   Remove the ramekins and let rest at room temperature for 30 minutes.

12   Remove the foil and serve.

Raspberry White Chocolate Bread Pudding

This decadent dessert mixes tart raspberries with smooth and creamy white chocolate in a gooey bread pudding. Calling for brioche bread, this rich afterthought won't be forgotten.

Serves 4 to 6

4 large eggs, beaten

½ teaspoon kosher salt

1 tablespoon fresh lemon juice

2 teaspoons vanilla extract

2 cups half-and-half

2 tablespoons unsalted butter, melted

1 cup sugar

2 cups cubed brioche

½ cup fresh or frozen raspberries, divided

4 ounces white chocolate, chopped, divided

1 Spray a 6-cup glass or metal bowl with nonstick cooking spray.

2 In a large bowl, whisk the eggs, kosher salt, lemon juice, vanilla, and half-and-half until combined.

3 Add the unsalted butter and whisk in the sugar and until dissolved.

4 Add the brioche, toss to combine with the custard mixture, and let sit for 5 minutes.

5 Pour half of the custard into the prepared bowl and top with ¼ cup of the raspberries and 2 ounces of the white chocolate.

6 Add the remaining custard and top with the remaining berries and chocolate.

7 Wrap the bowl with foil.

8 Place about 1 cup of water into the pressure cooker.

9 Place the foil-wrapped bowl into the pressure cooker; secure the lid.

10 When pressure is achieved, set a timer for 14 minutes.

11 When the cook time is complete and pressure is fully released, remove the lid with caution.

12 Using pot holders or tongs, carefully remove the bowl from the pressure cooker.

13 Carefully remove the foil from the bowl. Serve warm.

Blackberry Cream Cheese Coffee Cake

The beauty of the pressure cooker is its ability to cook food from fresh or frozen. So feel free to freeze your favorite berries at their best for future use. This recipe calls for blackberries, but I have a weakness for raspberries, too.

Serves 8

2 cups fresh or frozen blackberries

1 cup sugar

3 teaspoons quick-cooking tapioca

2 teaspoons orange zest, divided

8 ounces cream cheese, softened

One 16-ounce box pound cake mix

¼ cup whole milk

2 large eggs

1   Apply nonstick cooking spray to the pressure cooker.

2   In a medium bowl, combine the blackberries, sugar, tapioca, and 1 teaspoon of the orange zest; transfer to the pressure cooker.

3   In a food processor, combine the cream cheese, cake mix, milk, eggs, and the remaining 1 teaspoon orange zest; mix for 2 minutes, or until the batter is smooth.

4   Pour the batter over the blueberry mixture in the pressure cooker;secure the lid.

5   When pressure is achieved, set a timer for 20 minutes.

6   When the cook time is complete and pressure is fully released, remove the lid with caution.

7   Let cool for 20 minutes and invert onto a cake stand.

8   Serve warm or cold.

Creamy Cheesecake

This cheesecake is a canvas for any creation you'd like. Add fresh fruit and syrup for a tart twist or drizzle chocolate or caramel for an even richer taste.

Serves 4 to 6

¾ cup sugar

Two 8-ounce packages cream cheese

1 tablespoon fresh lemon juice

1 teaspoon vanilla extract

2 tablespoons all-purpose flour

1 cup sour cream

2 large eggs

1   Line a 6-inch spring form pan with parchment paper and apply nonstick cooking spray to the pan.

2   In a medium bowl, cream the sugar and cream cheese with a mixer until smooth.

3   Add the lemon juice, vanilla, flour, and sour cream to the cream cheese mixture.

4   Add the eggs, one at a time, and mix until smooth.

5   Pour the batter into the prepared pan and cover with aluminum foil.

6   Fit the pressure cooker with a stainless steel rack and add about 2 cups of water.

7   Place the spring form pan on the rack; secure the lid.

8   When pressure is achieved, set a timer for 30 minutes.

9   When the cook time is complete and pressure is fully released, remove the lid with caution.

10   Remove the cheesecake and let cool. Refrigerate for 3 hours before serving.

Brandy-Poached Apples

You'll be sure to impress your guests with these poached apples. They're even tastier served on top of vanilla ice cream.

Serves 6

6 firm Granny Smith apples, peeled

3 cups brandy

½ cup sugar

¼ cup honey

2 cups orange juice

1 cinnamon stick

1 star anise

1   Using a paring knife, cut a small hole in the bottom of each apple, and remove the seeds.

2   Cut the bottom of each apple so they will sit flat.

3   Add the brandy, sugar, honey, orange juice, cinnamon stick, and star anise to pressure cooker.

4   Place the apples into the pressure cooker; secure the lid.

5   When pressure is achieved, set a timer for 10 minutes.

6   When the cook time is complete and pressure is fully released, remove the lid with caution.

7   Gently transfer the apples to a platter.

8   With the lid off, set the pressure cooker to medium heat, and reduce the liquid for 20 minutes, or until thickened.

9   Pour the syrup over the apples and serve.

Cherry Cordial Bread Pudding

Though this recipe calls for brandy, you can leave it out if you prefer. The remaining ingredients will infuse this sure-to-please bread pudding with plenty of flavor.

Serves 6 to 8

6 ounces dried cherries

2 tablespoons brandy

4 large eggs, beaten

1½ cups heavy cream

½ cup brown sugar

1 teaspoon vanilla extract

1 cup chocolate chips

1 loaf challah bread, cubed and toasted

1   In a large bowl, soak the cherries in brandy for 5 minutes.

2   Add the eggs, cream, brown sugar, vanilla, chocolate chips, and challah to the bowl; mix well.

3   Apply nonstick cooking spray to the pressure cooker.

4   Transfer the contents of the bowl to the pressure cooker; secure the lid.

5   When pressure is achieved, set a timer for 15 minutes.

6   When the cook time is complete and pressure is fully released, remove the lid with caution.

7   Serve hot.

Creamy Quinoa Pudding

The vanilla brings the charm in this quinoa pudding. Use a paring knife to cut down the length of the vanilla pod, and use the dull side of the knife to scrape the contents of the pod into the pudding.

Serves 4 to 6

1 cup dry quinoa, rinsed

1 cup water

1½ cups rice milk

2 tablespoons agave syrup

Pinch of kosher salt

1 vanilla bean, split

¼ cup dried cherries

1   Place all of the ingredients into the pressure cooker; secure the lid.

2   When pressure is achieved, set a timer for 12 minutes.

3   When the cook time is complete and pressure is fully released, remove the lid with caution.

4   Remove vanilla bean and scrape the inside of the bean into the pudding.

5   Stir, top with fruit if desired, and serve immediately.

Healthy Rice Pudding

I opted for almond milk instead of the dairy variety in this super-simple recipe, making it totally vegan and ready in only 6 minutes.

Serves 6 to 8

4 cups cooks brown rice, cooked

4 cups almond milk

⅛ teaspoon kosher salt

½ cup sugar

1 cinnamon stick

¼ teaspoon nutmeg

½ cup raisins

1 tablespoon hazelnut liqueur

1   Place all of the ingredients into the pressure cooker; secure the lid.

2   When pressure is achieved, set a timer for 6 minutes.

3   When the cook time is complete and pressure is fully released, remove the lid with caution.

4   Top with dried fruit, if desired. Remove the cinnamon stick and serve immediately.

Dried Fruit Compote

Compote, the French word for "mixture," can be served warm or cold, over ice cream or alongside your favorite pork or chicken dishes.

Serves 4 to 6

1 pound dried apricots, cherries, or figs

1 cup orange juice

½ cup Amaretto liqueur

¼ cup sugar

1 cinnamon stick

1 teaspoon honey

1 Place all of the ingredients into the pressure cooker; secure the lid.

2 When pressure is achieved, set a timer for 5 minutes.

3 When the cook time is complete and pressure is fully released, remove the lid with caution.

4 Remove the cinnamon stick and serve.

Grandma's Bread Pudding

No one can do it like Grandma, but this may come in as a close second with this just-like-home bread pudding. Given its worldly nature, with popularity from Cuba to France, this dessert can complete any meal.

Serves 4 to 6

4 cups crusty bread, cut into 1-inch cubes

4 large eggs, beaten

1½ cups cream

1½ cups whole milk

½ cup sugar

1 tablespoon orange-flavored liqueur

1 teaspoon orange zest

1 teaspoon vanilla extract

¼ teaspoon kosher salt

½ cup dried cranberries

1   Spray a 2-quart stainless steel bowl or baking insert with nonstick cooking spray.

2   Place the bread cubes into the bowl.

3   In a separate medium bowl, combine the eggs, cream, milk, sugar, and orange liqueur; mix well.

4   Add the orange zest, vanilla, and kosher salt to the bowl; mix well.

5   Pour the egg mixture over the bread cubes and stir in the cranberries.

6   Cover the bowl with aluminum foil.

7   Pour about 2 cups of water into the pressure cooker and insert the bowl; secure the lid.

8   When pressure is achieved, set a timer for 15 minutes.

9   When the cook time is complete and pressure is fully released, remove the lid with caution.

10   Serve hot or cold.

Easy Flan

This recipe calls for the use of custard cups. These small glass dishes are traditionally used to serve desserts, but they also come in handy for sauces, separating ingredients, and side dishes. This easy flan is the happy ending to any meal.

Serves 6

½ cup sugar

½ cup water

1 (14-ounce) can sweetened condensed milk

1 (12-ounce) can evaporated milk

2 large eggs, beaten

2 large egg yolks

1 teaspoon vanilla extract

1 teaspoon orange zest

1 In a nonstick pan over high heat, combine the sugar and water and stir until the sugar is dissolved.

2 Reduce the heat to medium and let the sugar mixture cook for several minutes; do not stir.

3 When the water evaporates and the sugar turns a caramel color, remove from the heat. Divide the caramel among six 4-ounce custard cups; let rest for 10 minutes.

4 Pour about 1 cup of water into the pressure cooker.

5 In a bowl, combine the sweetened condensed milk, evaporated milk, eggs, egg yolks, vanilla, and orange zest; stir and pour into the custard cups.

6 Cover each cup with aluminum foil and stack the cups inside the pressure cooker; secure the lid.

7 When pressure is achieved, set a timer for 5 minutes.

8 When the cook time is complete and pressure is fully released, remove the lid with caution.

9 Remove the custard cups and chill until ready to serve.

Hot Fudge Cake

Amazing on its own, but to die for when topped with vanilla bean ice cream and hot fudge. This simple recipe turns your pressure cooker into an easy-bake oven!

Serves 8

One 18-ounce box chocolate fudge cake mix

1 cup heavy cream

3 large eggs

½ cup salted butter

1   Spray a 3-quart stainless steel bowl or baking insert with nonstick cooking spray.

2   Place all of the ingredients into a food processor, mix until smooth, and transfer to the bowl. Cover well with foil.

3   Pour about 2 cups of water into the pressure cooker and place the bowl in the water; secure the lid.

4   When pressure is achieved, set a timer for 30 minutes.

5   When the cook time is complete and pressure is fully released, remove the lid with caution.

6   Invert onto a cake stand and serve.

White Chocolate Cheesecake

This dessert needs no introduction; its name alone gets mouths watering. Pair this cheesecake with your favorite espresso for the utmost indulgence.

Serves 8

8 vanilla crème cookies

¼ cup slivered almonds

1 tablespoon unsalted butter

12 ounces cream cheese

¼ cup sugar

2 large eggs

1 teaspoon fresh lemon juice

1 teaspoon vanilla extract

4 ounces white chocolate, finely chopped

1 Preheat oven to 350°; place the cookies, almonds, and unsalted butter into a food processor fitted with metal S blade, then secure the lid.

2 Pulse for 1 minute, or until an even crumb is achieved.

3 Line the base of a 7-inch spring form pan with parchment paper; secure the ring around the pan, then apply nonstick cooking spray to the inside of the pan.

4 Press the cookie mixture into the bottom of the pan and bake for 10 minutes; let cool.

5 In a mixer or food processor, combine the cream cheese and sugar; mix until very smooth.

6 While mixing, add the eggs (one at a time) through the feed tube, then add the lemon juice, vanilla, and white chocolate. Mix until smooth, then transfer the mixture to the cooled spring form pan.

7 Wrap the pan tightly in aluminum foil; pour about 1 cup of water into the pressure cooker, then carefully place the pan into the pressure cooker and secure the lid.

8 When pressure is achieved, set a timer for 40 minutes.

9 When the cook time is complete and pressure is fully released, remove the lid with caution.

10 Carefully remove the pan from the pressure cooker.

11 Let rest at room temperature for 30 minutes, then refrigerate for 3 hours before serving.

Lemon Curd

Lemon curd is a great alternative to jam. Serve with your favorite bread or scone for afternoon tea or on top of pancakes or waffles for a scrumptious twist on brunch.

Serves 4 to 6

1¼ cups sugar

2 tablespoons lemon zest

½ cup lemon juice

⅓ cup unsalted butter, cut into small pieces

3 large egg yolks

3 large eggs

1   Place the sugar in the carafe of a blender and process until very fine, then transfer it to a 2-quart bowl.

2   Add the lemon zest, lemon juice, unsalted butter, egg yolks, and eggs to the bowl and beat, using a whisk, until well combined.

3   Cover the bowl tightly with aluminum foil.

4   Pour about 1 cup of water into the pressure cooker.

5   Place the bowl into the pressure cooker; secure the lid.

6   When pressure is achieved, set a timer for 13 minutes.

7   When the cook time is complete and pressure is fully released, remove the lid with caution.

8   Carefully remove the foil, then whisk the contents of the bowl well.

9   Refrigerate for 1 hour before serving.

Wine-Poached Pears

Your palate will be pleased by the sweet and savory complexity of this infusion. Serve over ice cream or a spoon of mascarpone cheese.

Serves 4 to 6

One 750-milliliter bottle port wine

4 Bartlett pears, peeled

3 sprigs fresh rosemary

½ teaspoon whole black peppercorns

1   Pour the wine into the pressure cooker.

2   Using a melon baller, core the bottom of each pear.

3   Cut off the bottom of each pear so they sit flat.

4   Place the pears into the pressure cooker.

5   Add the rosemary and peppercorns to the pressure cooker; secure the lid.

6   When pressure is achieved, set a timer for 10 minutes.

7   When the cook time is complete and pressure is fully released, open the lid with caution.

8   Remove the pears and transfer them to a platter.

9   To reduce the liquid in the pressure cooker, turn the pressure cooker on and set the timer for 10 minutes.

10 Remove the rosemary sprigs, and cook with the lid off until liquid turns into a syrup.

11 Top the pears with the syrup and serve.

Key Lime Cheesecake

Key lime, a Florida Keys favorite, makes this tart cheesecake the perfect summer treat. Don't worry, you don't need a citrus tree in your backyard to create this yummy dessert. The ingredients are easy to find year-round.

Serves 6 to 8

CRUST

10 vanilla crème wafers

2 tablespoons unsalted butter

¼ cup macadamia nuts

CHEESECAKE

Three 8-ounce packages cream cheese, softened

1 tablespoon all-purpose flour

One 14-ounce can sweetened condensed milk

3 large eggs

⅓ cup key lime juice

1 teaspoon lime zest

2 drops green food coloring (optional)

1 Preheat oven to 350°F; line the base of a 7-inch spring form pan with parchment paper, secure the ring around the pan, and then apply nonstick cooking spray to the inside of the pan.

2 For the crust: Place all of the ingredients into a food processor and process until smooth; press the mixture into the base of the spring form pan and bake for 10 minutes.

3 For the cheesecake: Place the cream cheese, flour, and sweetened condensed milk into the food processor; process for 1 minute or until very smooth; while processing, add the eggs, one at a time, through the feed tube, and then continue to process for 30 more seconds.

4 Add the key lime juice, lime zest, and food coloring (if using), and then process for an additional 30 seconds.

5 Pour the filling into the baked crust, then wrap the spring form pan in aluminum foil.

6 Pour about 1 cup of water into the pressure cooker, then carefully place the pan into the pressure cooker; secure the lid.

7 When pressure is achieved, set a timer for 40 minutes.

8 When the cook time is complete and pressure is fully released, remove the lid with caution.

9 Remove the pan from the pressure cooker using tongs and let cool at room temperature for 30 minutes.

10 Refrigerate the covered cheesecake for 2 hours before serving.

Poached Oranges

These beautiful oranges are great served on their own, but they're also super-delicious on a salad or as a garnish for your next pork roast.

Serves 4

4 large navel oranges, peeled

1 cup Amaretto liqueur

1 cup orange juice

½ cup sugar

1 star anise

1   Place all of the ingredients into the pressure cooker; secure the lid.

2   When pressure is achieved, set a timer for 5 minutes.

3   When the cook time is complete and pressure is fully released, remove the lid with caution.

4   Transfer the oranges to a platter.

5   With the lid off, set the pressure cooker to medium heat, and cook until liquid thickens.

6   Remove the star anise and pour the liquid over the oranges.

7   Serve immediately.

Coconut Soup

This Asian dessert will delight your taste buds and the small tapioca pearls will bubble on your tongue. The melon balls enhance the soup with added texture.

Serves 4 to 6

Two 13.5-ounce cans light coconut milk

½ cup small pearl tapioca

½ cup sugar

½ teaspoon kosher salt

1 cup ½-inch cantaloupe balls

1 cup ½-inch honeydew balls

1 Place the coconut milk, tapioca, sugar, and kosher salt into the pressure cooker; secure the lid.

2 When pressure is achieved, set a timer for 6 minutes.

3 When the cook time is complete and pressure is fully released, remove the lid with caution.

4 Chill the soup for at least 30 minutes.

5 Divide the soup among chilled bowls, then divide the melon balls and add to the bowls.

6 Serve at once.

Stuffed Apples

There's nothing like the smell of apples and cinnamon in the fall air. This sweet treat does double-duty, filling your home with its swirling aroma and hitting your taste buds with spicy-sweet flavor.

Serves 4

½ cup brown sugar

3 tablespoons unsalted butter, softened

1 teaspoon apple pie spice

2 tablespoons oats

4 small apples, cored

1 cinnamon stick

1 cup orange juice

1 In a medium bowl, combine the brown sugar, unsalted butter, apple spice, and oats; mix well.

2 Stuff each apple with the oat mixture.

3 Place the cinnamon stick and orange juice into the pressure cooker.

4 Add the apples to the pressure cooker; secure the lid.

5 When pressure is achieved, set a timer for 3 minutes.

6 When the cook time is complete and pressure is fully released, remove the lid with caution.

7 Serve immediately.

Pressure Cooker Measurement Chart

Please use the chart below for your reference.

INGREDIENT	AMOUNT	TIME SUGGESTED (minutes)	LIQUID REQUIRED (cups)
Vegetables			
Artichokes, trimmed	3 medium	14	2
Beans, black, dried	1 cup	12	2
Beans, navy, dried	1 cup	8	2 - 2½
Beans, pinto, dried	1 cup	15	3
Beans, red kidney, dried	1 cup	20	3½
Beans, string	1 lb	3	1
Beets	6 med	15	2
Cabbage head, quartered	1 med	10	2
Carrots, 2-inch pieces	2 cups	5	1
Corn on the cob	6 ears	4	1½
Parsnips, cubed	2 cups	4	1½
Squash, acorn, halved	4 halves	13	2
Squash, butternut, ½-inch slices	8 slices	4	1½
Meats, Poultry, Seafood			
Beef brisket	3 lbs	90	2–3
Beef ribs	6 whole	30	2
Chicken, boneless, skinless pieces, frozen	4lbs	5	2
Chicken, legs	4 whole	20	2
Chicken, whole, quartered	1 whole	20	2
Chicken, whole	3 lbs	20	3
Chuck roast	3 lbs	75	2–3
Corned beef	3 lbs	90	3
Baby back ribs	2 slabs	20	2
Lamb shanks	2 to 3 lbs	30	2
Pork chops (8 to 10 ounces each)	3 to 4	12	2
Pork loin	2 lbs	22	3
Short ribs	3 lbs	35	2
Spare ribs	1 slab	30	2
Stew meat, 1-inch pieces	3 lbs	18	4
Turkey breast	5 lbs	45	3
Veal shanks (8 ounces each)	3	30	2
Potatoes			
Potatoes, baking	4 large	15	2
Potatoes, red bliss	up to 20	7	2
Potatoes, white, cubed	3 cups	5	½

✳

DEBRA MURRAY, named a "home cooking evangelist" by the Tampa Bay Times, is the sweetheart of on-air food demonstration. She has appeared on TV in more than 85 million homes since 1998. Of the many celebrity chefs with whom she's worked, Debra currently does food styling and appears on EVINE Live with Todd English and Paula Deen. Debra shares the same enthusiasm as her viewers–spending her weekends conjuring up new recipes, mailing signed books, and interacting with her fans online. Having had a passion for food from a young age, perfecting cooking is more than just a job for Debra–it's what makes her tick. Debra Murray resides in Tampa, Florida.

Index